QUANTUM MECHANICS FOR YOUR SOUL

HOW TO REPAIR YOURSELF
AND SAVE THE WORLD AT THE SAME TIME!

ABOUT THIS BOOK

There is a world, within the world you know, and it's one that we are all looking for! Unfortunately, talking about it and wishing for it is a waste of time! Instead, I'm going to give you the tools to find it for yourself.

Better than that! This book is an antidote to the corrosive worldview that has left so many people doped up, alone and suicidal. Looking around at the world it is obvious that nothing is more damaging to the human mind than the belief that life is meaningless.

This book offers you coherent and scientific reasons to believe in a world where you are connected to everything and that every life has meaning. Finally, you will be able to ditch the platitudes and empty promises of 'New Age' spirituality and embrace your own truth.

Because here's the thing, the truth and light that you are searching for doesn't live in gurus, religions and cults (or me!).

Throughout history, human beings have seen that same truth and light within an almost infinite variety of 'things', but we would never have been able to see it '*out there*' if it didn't first exist within us. This book is uniquely and profoundly different because it fundamentally believes in the truth that exists within you!

Antonio Sebastian has spent over half a century searching for the answers to human suffering. His career as an engineer in the offshore and subsea industry gave him the freedom to travel and to study all over the world. Today, he is a philosopher, teacher and bestselling author. Join Antonio on a spiritual journey and find the secrets of the universe on a flight between Azerbaijan and the North Sea. But remember, this is one spiritual journey that is definitely 'down-to-Earth'!

TECHNICAL NOTE

The term 'Quantum' is used in this book to express the idea of a universal sub-atomic reality. It is not used to describe Einstein's doctrine of 'discrete separate particles' or quanta; neither is the term used to suggest a 'holographic' universe.

REFERENCES

All references are listed in chapter 16 and are separated into the relevant chapters. You will notice that some of my more outrageous comments have a number at the end of the sentence and are set in parenthesis. Please use this number to find the relevant detail in chapter 16.

ON A PERSONAL NOTE

I would just like to thank my darling wife, who also happens to be the reluctant co-author of this book. Her suggestions and amendments form the best of all my work; however, any remaining mistakes are entirely mine. She is also the most aggressive editor in the history of written communication. Without her, this work would have been effectively unreadable. Whatever good I have achieved in life is due to her, the rest is best forgotten.

****

BECAUSE SOMETIMES A BOOK IS NOT ENOUGH!

Whatever you get out of this book will largely depend on what you are looking for and what truth already lies within you.

In many ways, this book is a map of the world that exists within the world you think you know. If you are, indeed, one of those who search for that hidden reality, you're going to need a *guide* as well as a map.

It is for this reason that we encourage you to download the *28 Day Multimedia Foundation Course that accompanies this book.* It only takes ten minutes a day to turn your life around. The 28 Multimedia Foundation Course includes:

- *Course Calendar (Day-by-Day guidance)*
- *Course Manual*
- *Step-by-Step Meditation Manual*
- *Course Workbook*
- *Course Questionnaires*
- *Four Video Lessons*
- *Private Online Forum for all students*
- *Private Facebook Group to ask questions*
- *Access to a worldwide community*

The Foundation Course would normally be priced at $297 due to the quality and quantity of the materials but we decided that we wanted to help as many people as possible so, while we can, we will be giving the course away *FREE* with this book.

You will need the code listed at the end of this book in order to claim your FREE copy of the 28 Day Multimedia Course. Visit our website and click on the 'courses' tab and choose 'foundation course'. Enter the code when requested.

www.howdoifixme.com

Quantum Mechanics For Your Soul

How to Repair Yourself and Save the World at the Same Time!

CONTENTS

IS THIS BOOK FOR YOU?

How many times have you found yourself, in an airport, scanning rows of brightly coloured 'self-help' books, all of which promise to give you the life of the man with a twenty-thousand dollar suit and a smile like a white picket fence?

You know the books, they start with lines like, 'Imagine that you're as rich as me!' or 'I was flying my Jet helicopter to one of my talks'. Perhaps it's because each of these books appear more banal and incoherent than the last, the writers now compete for your attention by using the word 'F##K' as many times as possible.

Waiting for a delayed flight, looking for some kind of hope, you scan the contents of these books and feel something, deep down inside of your soul, shrivel up and die.

You know that you're looking for something but you're just not sure what; so you move on to the section marked 'New Age & Spirituality' in the faint hope that there might be something new.

You sigh and quickly put the book down when you realise that yet another impossibly named author has rehashed the same Dr Feelgood BS we've been reading since 1968.

The subtext of these books is always the same, 'you are not good enough'! 'You need to be more like me'! 'Buy my secret'!

The formula is always: YOU + SOMETHING ELSE = HAPPINESS

Relax! This book is nothing like that!

This book is different in every possible way. Why? Because it believes in *you*!

So why does that idea sound so remarkable?

Why do we read that statement and doubt its honesty?

Because for your whole life you've been lied to, we all have, and we've all become addicted to that lie. I can prove it. Let me show you the evidence.

MORE 'SELF = GOOD!

They tell you that if only you had more 'self', if only you had more 'belief' then finally you would be 'happy'. If only you could learn to NOT give a F##K about anyone but yourself, then you would be as free as they claim to be.

If this were true then the people with all the *'self'* should be the happiest people on the planet!

Sadly, we only have to watch the TV or read the news to know that this proposition is just not true. We see the rich and the famous, we see the sexual abuse, the addictions, the smug hypocrisy, the divorces, the suicides and we can see that they are even more miserable than we are.

So just having more 'self' can't be the answer we're looking for!

NEGATIVITY = BAD!

The self-help gurus always say 'Don't be negative!' 'Stay away from negative people!' 'Avoid negative energy!'

That's fine in principal but they don't explain what 'negativity' is and, to be honest, I'm pretty sure that they don't really know!

The dictionary says that negativity is being 'sceptical and pessimistic'.

So, according to Mr Twenty-thousand dollar suit, the secret of his success is his ability to maintain unshakable 'self-belief' and optimism.

In fact, we've gone so far down the 'self-belief' road that most gurus tell us that the secret to eternal happiness and personal success is to 'NOT give a F##K about anything'! (Believe it or not that's a quote.)

In theory, not giving a F##K about anything sounds fun but deep in our heart the alarm bells are going off!

There's a good reason why sane people find that proposition a bit disturbing! Unshakeable 'self-belief' and unwavering optimism are the hallmarks of mental illness. They are the most common emotional attributes of the sociopath (1).

Adolf Hitler never lacked 'self-belief'; in fact, his optimism verged on the delusional. Invading Poland was certainly a great example of someone not giving a F##K!

Unlimited 'self-belief' isn't the answer then!

SPIRITUAL NEED IN THE NEW AGE

In many ways, airports are like temples dedicated to the gods of materialism. The New Age section in the airport bookstore is a testament to our stubborn and heretical desire to believe in the world our new gods replaced.

Despite the fact that spirituality is now the crime that most of us won't admit to in public, there seems to be an unquenchable thirst for some kind of spiritual connection to 'something'.

These days you can buy Zen without effort and runes without the pagan sacrifice. Witchcraft without blood and spiritualism without the séance. Divorced from history, culture or context, New Age spirituality seems to be a Walt Disney version of something much deeper and much older.

From holy water that's supposed to cure cancer, to engraved brass boxes that will grant your every wish, the 'New Age' and 'self-help' market is full of people who grow incredibly rich selling us hope.

Our governments and their scientists tell us that we are just machines and that our lives are empty of all meaning but, despite a lifetime of indoctrination, we continue to buy the books that allow us to believe in a kinder world.

We search for some kind of meaning, whilst we live in world without joy. We hand over our money to Mr Twenty-Thousand Dollar Suit but we don't really believe in him, not really, but we keep looking all the same!

SOMETHING INSIDE IS BROKEN

Don't get me wrong, I'm not going to waste your time! I'm not saying that there's nothing wrong with life, because obviously there is!

We both know that you're looking for something!

It might be that what you're looking for you can't explain but deep down you feel it.

It feels like there's something fundamentally wrong with the world we live in.

You don't know what it is but it's there, like a splinter in your mind.

That splinter can cause all kinds of problems:

- *Your relationships feel superficial or dislocated. You can't connect to people in a meaningful way.*
- *You struggle emotionally with depression, anxiety or anger.*
- *You can't seem to get your career to take off. You have no confidence.*
- *Life feels empty and meaningless.*
- *The world is full of cruelty and unkindness.*
- *You cling to your addictions as if you were drowning..*
- *It feels like the Earth is dying.*

Human suffering takes many forms. For each of us it appears to be so different and unique. We all feel like our pain is exclusive to us, but it's not.

The itch you can't scratch, that's driving you mad, is the intuitive awareness that the world you see around you is not the same as the world you feel exists in your heart.

I want to let you into a secret. You're right!

The world around you is the lie that has been pulled over your eyes to blind you to the truth of who and what you really are. You can't see the truth because you've been conned into looking in the wrong direction.

THE KANSAS CITY SHUFFLE

You know the con? They get you to look left when you should be looking right.

We think the pea is under the cup on the left when really it was in the bad-man's hand. The big joke, the irony of this game, is that it's our own certainty and greed that eventually destroys us.

The reason that we don't trust our intuitive awareness, our heart and common sense, is because we've been programmed to look at life all wrong. We've been trained to believe what we are *told* to believe and not what we *know* is true.

For the last two hundred years, we've been brainwashed (literally) into looking for happiness in the wrong place.

Just like the God of Hollywood, Harvey Weinstein, we've been taught that we need more 'stuff' to make us happy in a world where the 'self' is king.

We've been conned into thinking that something outside of ourselves will make us happy.

So we've come to believe that if we don't feel happy it must be the fault of something outside of ourselves; we ditch the wife/husband/children and look for happiness elsewhere.

If that doesn't work we try to anaesthetise ourselves with sex, drugs or booze. We do anything to take our mind off the pain of life.

Eventually we go to the doctor and he gives us a drug so we can, at least, feel 'normal' again, but we never do, not for long. Almost inevitably, in one way or another, so many people kill themselves, not because they want to die but because they don't want the life they've got!

How did life get so messed up?

A CORROSIVE WORLDVIEW

'Materialism' is the doctrine that only 'matter' is real. Towards the end of the twentieth century it became a religion and is now enforced with all the power of the state. For the last hundred years, in the name of progress, life has been systematically stripped of all its beauty.

Today, children are indoctrinated to believe that their life is an accident and has no purpose. According to the 'experts' the universe doesn't give a F##K about us (to quote a recent guru's words).

This is the reason why one in five Americans are on some kind of prescribed psychotropic drug.

Anti-depressants are the reason that mass murder has become our latest spectator sport and materialism is the reason why suicide is the second biggest killer of young people; it has robbed them of all hope.

There is nothing more damaging to the human psyche than the belief that their life is meaningless.

The materialist worldview subliminally convinces us of three things: We are **alone** and **helpless** in the face of an **indifferent universe**.

If we feel unhappy we go shopping or change our job, car, house, partner, or children.

The materialist answer to suffering is always ME + Something else = Happiness. But that prescription is a little like taking a laxative to cure food poisoning. It kinda makes things worse!

"So how did we come to believe something so obviously not true?" I can hear you ask.

The only way that the materialist worldview can be supported is if we all agree to ignore the world we see and feel around us. We have to ignore so much of human experience that it is literally driving our civilisation insane.

"Why would we do such a thing!"

The answer is we were running from something even worse, or so we thought!

"IT'S RELIGION JIM BUT NOT AS WE KNOW IT!"

All religions are based, more or less, on the same premise that only the spirit is real.

Since the dawn of time, there has always been a man in a twenty-thousand dollar suit waiting to take advantage of your need to find meaning in your life.

He might be a prophet or a priest. He might look like a millionaire or a tramp but whatever shape these shysters take, they all have the same answer:

"There's something wrong with you and only I have the cure!"

All religions and self-improvement systems demand that you add whatever it is they're selling to your 'idea' of you. Just like materialism, religions offer us the same formula with a different twist:

You + something else = salvation.

Inevitably, the guru or prophet has the secret, the power or the keys to the kingdom and they will give it to you in return for your faith and your money.

None of these paradigms present a coherent model of reality that can be verified by you, through observation of the world around you; that's why religions tend to kill people who ask questions.

But just because they are not totally right, that doesn't mean that they're totally wrong.

UNIVERSAL AWARENESS OF INNER REALITY

At this point, you may sniff and say that spirituality is just for the weak minded and, indeed, that is the dogma of the materialist. You may argue, the opposite view, and insist that 'god' can only be found in a book and that is the position of most religions.

The strange truth is that both of these, often argued, positions entirely ignore the possibility that we are already subconsciously plugged into a universal sub-atomic reality.

Maybe that sub-atomic reality is something like gravity, easy to ignore until you fall over.

Maybe truth is already written on our very essence and books are only a distraction.

It would seem that independent scientific evidence is pointing, very strongly, in that direction.

As an example, you may have noticed that over the last twenty years a strange urban phenomenon has sprung up on our roads.

Today, in most Western countries, you can't seem to drive more than a few miles without seeing a sad and orphaned shrine of dying flowers and rotting cuddly toys left by the side of the road. These shrines seem to appear overnight, at the site of each car crash, as if by magic.

It is obvious that these bereaved and tormented people are expressing a connection to an inner reality that our strictly material society gives them no way to express or explore. It's almost as though they are ashamed of their own inner reality.

Maybe we are like the three blind men cleaning an elephant. Asked to describe the elephant, the man who cleaned the tail would say that an elephant was something like a snake. The man who cleaned the leg would say that an elephant was like a tree and the man who cleaned the sides would say an elephant was like a wall.

None of them would be entirely wrong but neither would they be entirely right. From Islam to Communism, Christianity to Atheism, underneath it all, what is it that we're looking for?

What inner vision is it that each of us seeks to validate?

For the first time in two thousand years, it might be time to talk about what connects us instead of what divides us. We've all been so busy fighting over our particular piece of the elephant that we refuse to talk about the elephant in the room: an inner reality that connects us all.

Maybe we are all connected to the same thing but we've just not cleaned enough parts to have an accurate picture yet?

IS KUNG FU A GOD?

In the 1970s everyone fell in love with kung fu. In a kind of positive racism, everyone in the West assumed that everyone in the East knew kung fu. We didn't care if you were Chinese, Japanese or Korean; as long as you were oriental we wanted to study with you.

The same was true for our thirst for Buddhism and Eastern philosophy. A lot of people, including myself, went to the Orient to study in monasteries.

My search for a cure to human suffering began before I was nine years old with the Bhagavad Gita and the Upanishads. My first Kensho (enlightenment experience) happened before my eleventh birthday. I've studied everything from Islam to Buddhism, Christianity to the Occult, Judaism to Kabbalah. I've travelled all over the world and studied in monasteries in England, Vietnam and Sri Lanka and here's the thing:

All human beliefs, from Islam to Atheism and from Christianity to Buddhism are just like different coloured pieces in a jigsaw. The great cosmic joke is that the universal truth we all seek can only be found within the cracks between the pieces but never within the pieces themselves.

We don't see that truth because we are so busy hanging on to our own piece of the jigsaw.

People say that Islam is a religion of peace despite all the evidence to the contrary simply because we all agree that it should be. People approve of Atheism because it professes a belief in humanity, despite the fact that it and its derivatives are collectively responsible for the deaths of 94 million people (2).

We all subconsciously believe in peace and love but those things only ever really exists inside of us not within the things we project them on to.

This is an important concept so let me explain.

TRANSFERENCE OF ENLIGHTENMENT

What do Christ, Muhammad, Richard Dawkins, Karl Marx and the Dalai Lama have in common?

Each of these men are revered by the masses for being the repository of some kind of transcendental truth. People look to them as 'gate keepers' or as sources of some kind of wisdom to which the common herd do not have access. Any evidence to the contrary is either ignored or dismissed.

Some of the words attributed to these men are quite clever, but a lot of their sayings don't make a lot of objective sense. Nevertheless people go on, year after year, playing a kind of philosophical ping-pong on behalf of their chosen 'gate keeper'.

Why do so many people attribute a wisdom and a clarity to each of these men that is evidentially greater than the sum of their words or their actions?

This process of 'Transference' or 'Projection' (as Sigmund Fraud and Carl Jung named the process) is the same as the 'assumption' of wisdom that my friends and I invested in our 'idea' of kung fu and all things oriental (3). It is evident that, throughout history, human beings 'transfer' or 'project' a concept of pure wisdom onto various people and cultures. It would follow that this universal and timeless wisdom must therefore first exist within us.

For the sake of clarity, let's call this indwelling and universal wisdom 'Holistic Enlightenment' and it is the shadow of our own holistic enlightenment that we, as individuals and as a culture, see projected outward onto the world around us.

The people, societies, religions or objects that we invest with this quality are incredibly diverse, but on investigation none of them possess holistic enlightenment in or of themselves.

This is the big clue! Obviously, you can't project onto the world a quality that you don't already possess.

It is absolutely vital that you understand this concept so, in order to be clear, let me try to explain it in a slightly different way.

IF I'M COLOUR BLIND DOES RED EXIST?

For instance, if you were born blind to the colour 'red' then effectively, for you, that colour does not exist. Indeed, you would not be able to even imagine what a red rose would look like.

For people to instinctively resonate with the wisdom of Christ or Dawkins that wisdom must exist first in our own hearts and it is therefore a wisdom we all share.

The QM4YS system will demonstrate that this quality of 'Holistic Enlightenment' is common to all living beings.

The splinter in your mind that has been driving you mad is the disconnect between your subconscious connection to this universal reality and the world of suffering around you.

We all KNOW that there is something wrong with the world, because deep in our hearts we all know exactly how life should be. Therefore, in reality, "You are the only one who can fix you."

SCIENCE PROVES THAT YOUR HEART IS RIGHT

So materialism has become a corrosive worldview but it didn't screw us over on its own. It had help!

Once upon a time, the Spanish Inquisition controlled all of Christendom. A privileged non-military elite were able to control a vast population by dictating to the people what questions could be asked and, more importantly, what questions could not. Ultimately, the Church decided what was true and what wasn't.

Today, 'science' decides what questions can be asked and which questions can't.

Once upon a time, during the Enlightenment, scientists were largely self-funded and were free to follow their curiosity and the evidence toward a conclusion. Today, not so much!

When I was young, 'scientists' were falling over themselves to convince us that smoking cigarettes was a good thing. Now they won't shut up about how bad it is.

If I've learnt anything in half a century it is that you can pay a 'scientist' or a car salesman to say anything. Scientists today rely on funding from governments and big business, and change their opinions to suit the whims of their masters.

For obvious reasons, during the Enlightenment, we all decided that it would be a jolly good idea if the Church were separated from the power of the State and that worked well for awhile.

Unfortunately, 'science' has become a new religion and at the same time a prisoner of its own success. Today, if you're a real scientist and you have an original idea, which threatens the consensus, you won't get funding. If you independently publish your results your career will be ruined. They will hunt you down like a rabid dog (4).

As a technical authority working with electromagnetics in the power generation industry, I had a unique opportunity to study the work of several independent scientists working in fields that would not often normally communicate. It was immediately obvious to me that each of these remarkable men were cleaning different parts of the same elephant.

The 'elephant' that all of these men are working on is a 'sub-atomic' reality that explains the world that we've all been taught to ignore.

What is more important is that this 'elephant' looks an awful lot like the 'something' we've all been looking for.

THE HOLISTIC UNIVERSE

Throughout history, in different cultures and at different times, people have had different legends and myths about the sun. None of those stories actually change the nature of the sun. The sun is an objective reality and a fact of our lives.

We could argue over which story about the sun is 'true' but ultimately the only story about the sun that matters is your own.

We can swap observations and ideas but in the end, my vision of the sun should never replace your own.

Similarly, the universal reality that exists between the pieces of the jigsaw of your life, the Holistic Universe that we are all plugged into, is an objective reality and exists quite independently of your belief or your mental constructions.

Contrary to popular belief 'quantum', or to be more accurate sub-atomic reality, can be understood and experienced by all of us as an objective reality, and because of that, this book gives you scientific reasons to believe in, and understand, your own inner life.

Because ultimately you can't fix something if you don't know how it's made and how it got broke.

QUANTUM MECHANICS FOR YOUR SOUL (QM4YS)

The Quantum Mechanics for Your Soul (QM4YS) system will demonstrate that the world you always suspected existed really does. Contrary to popular belief, every atom in your body is connected to every other atom in the universe. Your life is of infinite importance to every living being and we are all connected to everything!

But this isn't a New Age book and this isn't a Dr Feelgood Meme! That universal truth, when you see it for yourself, changes everything. Once seen, it means that you have to accept the responsibility for being truly alive. Finally you will be able to begin to understand the mechanism of human suffering and evolution.

The QM4YS system gives you a way to fix yourself and the world around you.

SO WHAT DOES THE 'QM4YS' SYSTEM GIVE ME?

This book, and the multimedia 28 day foundation course that comes with it, deals with the profound implications of this universal reality.

After studying this book you will understand how to:

- Overcome depression, anxiety and addictions.
- Stop chasing temporary happiness and finding yourself paying for it full time.
- Find lasting fulfilment.
- Begin to live 'in the moment'.

- Connect to people on a genuine level.

- Learn to 'treasure' what you have and find value in every moment.

- Start to be the cause and not the reaction to the events in your life.

- Learn to create a daily practice that will grow your happiness.

- Learn to understand how to 'get out of your own way' and start to live a fully conscious life.

For most people their inner life is a complete mystery to them. For that reason we often end up making ourselves and everyone around us miserable. The QM4YS system provides a way to enter into that inner sub-atomic reality in order to finally take control of our lives.

THE CIRCLE IS NOT A STRAIGHT LINE

I can't explain this unique system of self-repair as a straight line. I know, because I've been trying for years.

I'm an engineer, I like logical sequences. I look for A, which is followed by B, which leads to C.

Unfortunately, the sub-atomic world is not a mathematical theory; it is a physical reality that you can verify for yourself. The quantum world IS the natural world. But, here's the thing!

Nature doesn't do math!

The world 'out there' is made up of only two things, rhythm and spin.

You have to grasp this system like you would the punch line to a half forgotten joke: understanding will come when you are ready. Truth is not linear, it is more like an onion with meanings within meanings each helping to form and support all the others.

The important thing you need to realise is that the truth you will find at the end of this journey will not be mine, nor will it be the truth of some dead Greek philosopher. The truth that I am offering you is your own.

NEW HOPE

This book was born during a long-haul flight from Azerbaijan to Aberdeen. Somewhere between the Caspian and the North Sea, I realised that I had found an answer to human suffering within the world of Quantum Mechanics. It was an answer that needed to be shared with the world.

The challenge was to tell you enough that you could grasp the depth of the explanation but not too much as to bore you to death. Depending on your background and/or your prejudices, some of the sections in this book might prove a little too much or equally not enough. I hope that you will forgive me and realise that I've tried to write in a way that this book will help most people.

Come with me on that journey and I will try to peel away each layer of truth one by one. By the time we get to Aberdeen, I guarantee that you will have a new direction and a new way of seeing your life.

The QM4YS system is as old as the human race but it is not defined or limited to any culture or religion but has, from time to time been reflected in them.

This book discusses the foundational concepts of the QM4YS system of self-repair in a way that I hope you will find helpful and at times amusing. It will give you a way to fix yourself and more than that, it will give your life new hope.

In order to understand the reason why you suffer in your life, we need to visit Baku and the beginning of this journey.

****

CHAPTER 2

HAPPINESS ON A CORROSIVE PLANET

I could still smell oil as I stepped into the Heydar Aliyev Airport in Azerbaijan. It was the oil and tar oozing out of the ground that gave the country its name, 'The Land of Fire'.

It was from here that the Byzantine Empire obtained 'Greek Fire'. This secret weapon allowed Constantinople to defeat the invading Muslim hordes with what we would, today, call marinised Napalm.

It wasn't long ago that Azerbaijan was run by the Russians. Today, on the southern shore of the Caspian Sea, Baku is the hub that controls the country's oil production.

The airport sits like a stranded glass spacecraft on the plains just outside of the city. It is a wonder that the city is as beautiful as it is! Under Stalin, the Communist Party had killed thousands of the Azerbaijan engineers, teachers and intelligentsia. It's not surprising, then, that the airport buildings were designed by a Turkish company!

Karl Marx was a Russian Jew who came from a long line of Rabbis (1). Maybe it was his Jewish roots that gave him such a concern for the poor or maybe it fed his ego to the point that he thought he could tell everybody else in the world how to live! To date, the naive good intentions of Karl Marx has directly and indirectly cost over 94 million people their lives (2). You have to ask yourself why?

Marx's solution to human suffering and poverty was in no way original. In fact, 'sharing' has worked perfectly well, in the past, when the size of the communities were limited by the ties of kinship, tribe and clan. When a people are united by love and mutual interest, such a system might be a utopia. Why then, in over a hundred and fifty years, has Marx's system so spectacularly failed every time it has ever been tried?

The security guard glared at me as I tried to find my check-in. It was 04:00 hours but the terminal was already busy. It seemed like five hundred people were waiting to check-in just for my flight.

Predictably enough, the check-in system had no record of my company's booking so I was directed to speak to an 'official' in a military hat that looked big enough to be used as a table. As I stood at his counter trying to explain the problem to him, people kept leaning across me to grab his attention. In the end he could help no one!

I was beginning to see why Communism might have failed.

Why is it that despite our very best intentions, everything we think will make us happy never does in the long-term? In fact why do our best intentions seem to cause so much misery?

Obviously poor old Karl Marx made some fundamental mistakes in his calculations but he is not alone. For most of us, any kind of lasting happiness is so hard to find. Human suffering is a monster that just seems to creep up on us and knock life's ice-cream out of our hand as he runs away giggling.

We need to get a grip on this whole process of how to be happy. The truth is that most of us don't really understand 'suffering' and if you don't understand 'suffering' how can you possibly learn to be 'happy'?

AUTOMATIC REACTIONS

Most people go through their lives like robots. Something happens, which they perceive to be good for them, in the short-term, and they have pleasant feelings. Is that happiness?

Conversely, something happens to them that they perceive to be bad, in the short-term, and they feel unpleasant feelings. Is that suffering?

But wait! It gets even more confusing, not everything that is bad for us in the short-term is bad for us in the long-term. Like the redundancy that leads to new opportunities, or the divorce that leads to new love. Conversely, not everything that seems good in the short-term is good for you in the long-term. Like that extra bit of cake or that extra bottle of wine.

Are we on some kind of cosmic pinball machine being flipped by the accidents of life? Can anyone really explain the mechanism that creates human suffering and more importantly, the mechanism that creates happiness?

We betray our ignorance of our own inner life with the words we use to ask the question: "What MAKES you happy?" Can any 'thing' make us happy? Do 'things' come charged with happiness like some kind of electricity?

It follows that if we don't understand the rules we are never going to be able to truly play the game.

HAPPINESS IN AMERICA

Those of us born into the religion of materialism assume that the more stuff we get the happier we will be. Certainly anyone born after the mid-nineteen-fifties has been surrounded all of their lives with mass media telling them to consume more 'stuff'.

It is true that consumerism is the fuel that drives the engine of an industrialised nation but the question is, 'will it make us happy and if so why'?

If 'Natural Selection' is the motor that drives evolution, we might speculate that happiness is a chemical-driven pleasure that rewards our urge to reproduce our unique DNA. Therefore, it would follow that, evolution might reward the most successful individuals with a feeling we call 'happiness'.

But in the modern world, in polite society, if a man says that he has a hundred children he would be considered a freak.

If he spent all day at the sperm bank making deposits in a desperate bid to comply with Darwin's order to reproduce his DNA he would probably get arrested.

So for us in the West, we have substituted 'stuff' for the children we no longer want. We now use 'stuff' as a token of our evolutionary success instead of children. We live our lives to collect as much 'stuff' as possible as tokens of our evolutionary 'fitness'.

If this worldview is correct, we should be able to assume that the people with all the 'stuff', like the people with all the 'self' are the happiest people on the planet. As we have already seen, the rich and the famous are more miserable than the rest of us but we've been trained not to see it. We never do the math!

Nobody says, 'why am I killing myself to buy new stuff when these guys with all the stuff are more miserable than me'?

So like hamsters on a wheel we carry on running to nowhere: if we feel depressed we get a new job, car, house, partner, children and now we can even get a new gender. We are blinded to the truth because we assume that happiness is MADE by the things around us.

When a wife justifies leaving her husband by screaming, 'You just don't make me happy anymore!' What she is actually saying is that she expected her husband to come fully charged with unlimited happiness and now she wants a refund. Obviously, her husband's 'happiness' battery has run out and now she wants to replace him for one that's full.

So she will find someone new that will 'make' her happy! Morning television audiences will clap and shout 'You do you girl!' and whoop like a bunch of demented Sioux warriors. But like a game of musical chairs, eventually, you can't change anymore. You run out of tokens of your evolutionary success and eventually you have to sit in the seat life gave you and that can feel pretty uncomfortable.

SUFFERING VS. PAIN

Deepak Chopra says that, **'Suffering can be defined as that pain that makes life seem meaningless'.**

So Mr Chopra is saying that 'suffering' is a reaction to a certain kind of pain.

Like reversing sensors on your car, pain is just a feedback loop and is, in many ways, unavoidable and often very helpful. Some people who are born without a sense of pain end up constantly accidentally injuring themselves. Obviously then, 'suffering' is not just 'pain'.

Twenty-six centuries ago an Indian Prince named Gautama who later came to be called 'the Buddha', spoke in the language called Pali, in which he discussed this subject. He said that all human beings experience a thing called 'Dukkha'. This word is most often translated as 'suffering' but this is like saying arm wrestling is a form of boxing. You can't really translate Dukkha into English but you can kind of describe it. He said that there were three kinds of 'suffering':

1. *Pain* - we may experience this as old age, sickness and death.

2. *Impermanence* - we experience this when all the things we desire are subject to change. The people we love grow old and die. We leave the 'stuff' that we worked so hard to accumulate behind when we die or lose them to the IRS.

3. *Dependent Origination* - the centre of our world, the 'self', is entirely dependent on causes and has no inherent reality. This fact, in itself, he said brings suffering but does it?

As you will discover later in this book, points 1-3 are obviously a direct observation of the universal sub-atomic (Quantum) reality but they fail to explain the actual mechanism of human suffering. Impermanence and Dependent Origination only create suffering if they are viewed from the perspective of the 'Self of Now'. The Buddha turned his TV off too soon and kind of missed the point of the show!

Obviously, as you can imagine, Gautama Buddha didn't get invited to a lot of parties and I only include this information so that you have some context. It's important that you start to ask the question, 'how can we learn to be happy'?

I would suggest that the fundamental mechanism that creates 'suffering' and 'happiness' is much simpler than Gautama's explanation, but in order to understand the answer you first have to fully comprehend the question. So let's look at what we might mean when we say 'Human Suffering'.

In reality, our experience of suffering is caused by a collection of mechanisms over a lifetime:

- *Direct to self:* this might be something like the damage we do to our self when we indulge our greed or fantasies.

- *Direct to the world:* this might be something like the damage we do when we use violence or abuse someone. It might also be the affect our negative thoughts and feelings has on the people around us.

- *Directly on us by a second person:* this might be the suffering caused to us by family members as child abuse.

- *Indirectly on us by a second person:* this might be like someone killing themselves by throwing themselves in front of a train. You're late for work and lose your job.

- *Directly on us by cumulative events:* this might be the suffering of someone caught up in a civil war or political events.

- *Directly on us but due to our own primary cause:* the suffering we've caused returning to harm us: this is like Jeffrey Dahmer being beaten to death by an inmate or Harvey Weinstein having his career destroyed by a media feeding frenzy.

- *Empathic suffering:* this is caused by having to live in world that is dissonant with our inner life model. This is like having to live in a world full of cruelty and needless violence when you long for a world of kindness and love.

This, of course, is not an exhaustive list of the mechanisms by which we suffer, but it gives you some food for thought about your own experiences.

The mechanisms of suffering are reasonably obvious but the reason why one action causes suffering and another does not still eludes us. Buddha's use of the term 'Dukkha' and 'Karma' does not really offer us any clarification that we can use in our own lives.

IT IS WRITTEN

Every religion since time began has tried to come up with an answer to the question of human suffering. Religions try to deal with our suffering by telling us what is good and what is evil.

The implication of all religions is that 'suffering' is caused by doing what is 'evil'.

Some religions tell us not to kill, while others tell us that the only way to heaven is to kill in the name of God. One religion insists that we have free will but another demands that we submit. All religions tell us that, without them, we are condemned to hell.

Invariably all religions fail and for the same reason; they all tried to create an answer based on their own ideas and their own cultural and/or racial bias.

They all try to find 'God' in the written word rather than in the objective reality of their own lives.

The problem is how can we become aware of the objective reality of our own lives?

HAVE ZOMBIES TAKEN OVER THE WORLD?

Most people live their entire lives as a reaction and are, to all intents and purposes, entirely unconscious. If you live your life on autopilot are you really alive? When you talk to people who only react automatically are you really talking to them or their answer machines?

Take poor old Harvey Weinstein, the God of Hollywood, he had more stuff than anyone could shake a stick at but it wasn't enough to make him happy. He had an urge, a voice deep inside of him that made him want what other people could only dream of. He had a voice in his head that said that it was OK to abuse his position of power. Obviously he never questioned that voice. He lived his life as a reaction to urges and thoughts that he couldn't understand.

I'm sure that for most of his life that might have felt great! But all the time, for all of those years, he was damaging something deep inside of himself and leaving suffering out there in the world.

Eventually, the suffering, the humiliation and the hurt that he had caused rolled back over him like a tidal wave and destroyed his life and his legacy.

How do I know? Because I'm the same and so are you! We all are.

We all are victims of our deepest thoughts and urges, none of which we understand.

HAPPINESS ON A CORROSIVE PLANET

It is a fact of life that you can't fix your car if you don't know what's wrong. Most people go through life reacting automatically to the accidental events of their lives. Indeed, most people are so unaware that they don't even know how unaware they are.

The question of human suffering and how to find happiness has occupied the minds of philosophers and sages for thousands of years. Most of their answers are limited by their own cultural and personal bias and are therefore of no real use to us in the modern world.

In order to find a universal answer to the question of suffering we will have to examine objective reality and leave cultural fantasy behind us. Happiness can only be found in what is real.

We will only find those answers when we learn to see life, 'just as it is'. Unfortunately, in order to do that we need to learn to look at life in a completely different way.

MY FLIGHT IS CALLED

Check-in had been a nightmare! I'd finally realised that the only way to get attention was to act like I owned the airport. Shouting in a very superior and confident way seemed to work.

I'd finally got a ticket and made it through security just as the flight was called.

I could only get an economy ticket so resigned myself to a long wait. As it turned out, I was glad for the delay. I sat down to watch the show.

If you've ever seen a rugby match as some fool tries to run with the ball toward the posts pursued by a snarling pack of sweaty men you might be able to imagine the fate of the pretty air hostess as she opened the gate to the plane. She bravely tried to check the boarding pass of the first few attackers, but after getting elbowed aside she decided that discretion was the better part of valour.

The gate was now jammed by the bodies of middle-class businessmen. The urge to be first had resulted in nobody boarding the plane. The air hostess called for the pilot to come and enforce some kind of order. A small man with a big hat arrived. He had a voice like Vin Diesel, which seemed to be enough to calm the mob.

Twenty minutes later, I was shoehorned into an aisle seat.

Finally, I was on my way to Istanbul.

****

CHAPTER 3

A CORROSIVE WORLDVIEW

We were descending into Istanbul over Turkey and the view of the Bosporus was amazing.

My next flight was a connection to Düsseldorf, which was a bit of a detour but it was the only way my agent could get me to Aberdeen. I only had an hour and a half 'turnaround' so I was keen to get off the plane and into the terminal as quickly as possible.

Turkey seems such a nice country; looking down at the land below, it is hard to think that only a hundred years ago, the Armenian people had been ethnically cleansed from this country (1).

Between 1915 and 1923, over 1.5 million Armenians were killed by their Turk and Kurdish neighbours. How do you persuade good people to do such evil things?

History tells us that if you can manipulate people's belief then you can persuade them to do almost anything. The Armenian Genocide was a direct result of Turkish and Kurdish belief, not as individuals but as a people. Let me explain why this is relevant.

Have you ever seen a shoal of fish move as they try to escape from a predator? They move as if they were one being. The remarkable thing is that each fish is both an individual and a part of a collective 'hive-mind' all at the same time.

As a more practical example, you might say that individuals within the 'Young Turks' movement were very nice people and they may have been, but that doesn't change the nature of the atrocity committed against innocent Armenian women and children.

In Germany, until very recently, you could still talk with ex-members of the Nazi Party and most were perfectly nice individuals but that doesn't change what the Germans did as a group.

We can therefore say that there are two levels to our existence, individual and collective.

THE BLINDING POWER OF BELIEF

We create the world we live in through the stories we believe. Where we are as a society and where we are going is a product of our collective belief in a particular worldview.

When Cambodia won its independence from France it was a country of over 7 million people, most of whom were Buddhists. In 1975, the Khmer Rouge (Communist Red Army) took control of the country and tried to enforce a Stalinist regime overnight. It is estimated that 2.5 million people were murdered over a three-year reign of terror; a period we now call the 'Killing Fields' (2). Why would they do such a thing?

Belief is like a weight of water pushing us forward and the stories that the Cambodians grew up with put no value on life and, within that philosophical vacuum, Communism made perfect sense. Genocide does not require central organisation and nor does it need a conspiracy; it only needs a common collective belief.

Today, in the West, most people live a life of incredible luxury. Despite their material advantages, ordinary people are unhappier than they've ever been.

Suicide is the second biggest killer of young people in the West. Most young adults are on some form of psychotropic drug. Depression and anxiety are as common as fast food outlets. Why?

Here's the truth and you're not going to like it! People are miserable because everyone around them is so bloody unpleasant. Collectively people are shallow, narcissistic and cruel but it's not their fault.

For the last fifty years we have been told, by the establishment, that our lives are an accident. We have been robbed of all hope. Morality is subjective. There is no such thing as good and evil. Justice today is decided on social media.

That is a pretty depressing prospect for any teenager! With no moral datum and no one to look up to, apart from Kim Kardashian, all a young person can do is desperately try to signal their virtue and hope that it's one that the Twitter mob will approve of this week.

Instinctively people try to find a cure for their lives but are blinded by this collective worldview that has enslaved us all. From Christianity to Islam, Witchcraft to Aramaic Toning, nothing seems to work in the long-term and there's a very good reason why!

Imagine that the only water you have to drink comes from a poisoned well. Every time you get sick you go to the doctor and each time he gives you a different kind of medicine. Every time you feel a little better you start drinking the same poisoned water only to once again fall sick.

The well that has poisoned our lives and keeps us blind to the one cure that could save us is our collective belief in the materialistic worldview.

Now here's a secret that will change your life! That well didn't get poisoned on its own. It's not an accident that modern life is so corrosive.

When I was young, scientists were queuing up to convince us of the health benefits of smoking cigarettes. Most good restaurants used to have a bowl of cigarettes on the table. Smoking in-between courses was normal. Scientists knew that it would kill us but they kept quiet. Why?

When did our governments and consensus science become the enemy of ordinary people?

CONSENSUS SCIENCE IS THE WIZARD OF OZ

In the second half of the twentieth century, ordinary people believed in 'science', in our governments and in the benefits of materialistic consumerism. We believed that the 'doctor was always right' and that policemen were 'public servants'. In short, we trusted that the 'establishment' had our best interests at heart.

But, our naiveté has cost the world dearly.

Today, in this brave new world, all of us are condemned to live out our empty lives alone. We believe that our suffering is unique to us. We are told that we are 'depressed' or that we are Bi-Polar. Our symptoms become our identity.

Our relationships are temporary alliances rather than lifetime commitments. The only image of hope that we are now permitted is on some tampon commercial with a ukulele soundtrack and a really annoying cheerful whistle.

We all feel that there's something wrong with the world but we don't know what! The truth is that we are all trapped within the corrosive worldview our parents and grandparents left to us. We are lost and our only compass is pointing us in exactly the wrong direction: we have been trained to see the world entirely through the 'Self of Now'.

THE LONG WAR

For the last two hundred years, a secret war has been fought for the hearts and minds of the people. On the one hand, materialism tells us that there is nothing real that is not material. Confusingly, on the other hand, organised religions tell us that there is nothing real that is not spirit.

Religions only recognise the life of the spirit, while materialism won't even consider the possibility that there is such a thing.

Neither of these two worldviews have a good track record and it is an historical fact that they have both, whenever they've had the chance, created hell on Earth and still do!

However, once you deny materialism the quasi-religious status that it demands, the questions it has failed to answer present us with an opportunity to find a middle-way between these two toxic extremes.

Dogmatic religion just as much as dogmatic materialism obscures the truth of our lives by telling us exactly what questions can be asked and which can't.

Christianity insists that all life is inherently evil but ignores the evidence that children are born innocent.

The materialist professor insists that all consciousness is an illusion; an accidental product of natural selection but ignores his own inner life and the fact that forming an independent opinion demands independent thought.

I think it was the Dalai Lama himself that said, *'Transcendental truth cannot be found through logic but once found it should not, itself, contradict that logic'.*

It is not logical to insist that something isn't true just because you don't want it to be true. Both the materialist and the spiritualist models fail because they have to deny or ignore so much of the human experience and observable truth.

SEPARATION OF 'CONSENSUS SCIENCE' AND THE STATE

You've only got to look at European history to understand why it's a very good idea to separate the Church from the State. Unfortunately, nobody has yet realised that we desperately need to separate science from the State as well!

Just like Christianity, science has become a religion. More worryingly, it has also become a system of mass indoctrination. This virulent and aggressive form of 'science', which we will call 'consensus science' as a way to differentiate it from 'real science', has bullied the world into submission.

Please don't take my word for it! Try asking a question that challenges the consensus.

You will find that there are many questions that 'consensus science' will not allow. You will be told that your question is a non-question or that you wouldn't understand the answer.

More often than not you will be pointed to evidence that independent scientists have already debunked.

Consensus scientists are just a group of people who think they are better than everyone else. They don't like to listen to new ideas because they are too busy listening to their own opinions. They don't seem at all troubled by the questions they can't answer; they just call them 'illegal'.

If you know any consensus scientists, you may have noticed that they can often seem very narrow and dogmatic in their views.

Convincing us of the benefits of tobacco smoking wasn't the first time that scientists have betrayed the trust of the people and as it turns out it wasn't the last!

A GLOBAL ICE AGE

When I was young we were constantly being told by eminent scientists that the world was going into an Ice Age. In 1978, Leonard Nimoy (Mr Spock from Star Trek), narrated a documentary entitled, *'The Coming Ice Age'*. The 'scientists' at the National Oceanic and Atmospheric Administration (NOAA) were confidently predicting colder weather and an imminent disaster.

In fact, at the time, there was an 86% scientific consensus that the planet was on a cooling path.

William Connolley, a Green Party member, has since abused his Wikipedia Admin rights by rewriting thousands of Wikipedia articles in order to cover up this obvious gaff and give them the correct spin. The scandal of this fraud was exposed by Lawrence Solomon in the National Post (3).

Real scientists will provide evidence. Religious fanatics, on the other hand, will give you ad hominem attacks, emotion and opinion. Real scientists do not fake the evidence and they do not try to hide from their mistakes.

WOULD YOU LIKE AN ICE PICK WITH THAT?

In 1949, lobotomy was hailed by scientists as a medical miracle and Egas Moniz was awarded the Nobel Prize for inventing the procedure.

American psychiatrist, Dr Walter J. Freeman, took psychiatry to new depths of horror by giving people a lobotomy (destroying the frontal lobe of the brain) without anaesthetic through the simple expedient of sticking an ice pick through their eye socket into their brain. He travelled the country in his *'Lobotomobile'* giving America the benefit of his extensive 'education' and services at $25 a go!

By the time Freeman retired at 57 he had lobotomised over 3500 people, some as young as four years old. He had no surgical training and over 25% of his patients ended up in a vegetative state and many died. He even lobotomised John F. Kennedy's sister, Rosemary, and left her with severe brain damage. You could never accuse psychiatrists of being faint hearted (4).

Even today scientists come up with new ways to destroy parts of your brain in order to make you docile but never as a way to improve your life.

CHEMICAL LOBOTOMY

Scientists enthusiastically carried on with the mutilation of their patients regardless of the damage they caused to them or their families. After all, they were the new 'priesthood'.

By the 1950s psychiatrists had discovered that a chemical, originally designed to kill parasites in pigs, could be repackaged as a chemical lobotomy.

Thorazine was a much neater solution than an ice pick and it gave the profession an entry into the drug industry.

What they didn't tell their patients was that their new wonder 'cure' often caused long term or permanent brain damage (5).

And so it was that a marriage made in hell began, the psychiatry industry had finally met the pharmaceutical industry; it was love at first sight — the world would never be the same again. The drugging of the world had begun!

A MEDICATED WORLD

Very quickly, psychiatry became an industry of drug pushers. In order to justify the continued use of drugs, a medical report was fabricated that stated (the new dogma) that all mental disorders were caused by a 'chemical imbalance' in the brain.

Dr Mark Filidei, a director of a medical clinic is on record saying that *"there is no chemical test to show a chemical imbalance related to any psychiatric disease."*

Dr Peter R. Breggin has testified in court that drug companies falsified the data regarding chemical imbalances in the brain and hid the evidence that their drugs cause depression and suicidality (6).

In the face of mounting evidence of the harm these drugs do, the F.D.A. eventually called a hearing — Prozac was in the dock. Witness after witness was called but they couldn't find a psychiatrist that didn't have a financial agreement with the drug companies.

In 1997, the drug companies were finally given permission to advertise to the public directly. Prescriptions shot through the roof but so has incidence of suicide and murder. Eventually anti-depressants had to be labelled with a warning to say that they could cause suicidal behaviour. Although psychiatrists might argue that suicide does in fact cure depression.

NEVER MIND THE BABY

Thalidomide was licensed for use in the UK in 1958. German scientists had punted it out as a sedative, a sleeping pill, and an aid for pregnant mothers suffering from morning sickness. The drug was sold as being completely safe for everyone including a mother or a child. Its sales nearly matched those of aspirin.

Unfortunately, due to the affects of the drug, children were born with no limbs at all or flippers like a fish. When I was young, children with no arms were common.

Nobody really knows how many lives the Thalidomide drug damaged, as the scientists and the establishment have colluded in order to hide the extent of the suffering. They never even bothered counting how many miscarriages the drug caused.

Gruenenthal was the German company that produced this drug and had a leading role in Nazi Germany. They employed Dr Heinrich Mueckter as chief scientist. Dr Mueckter was wanted in Poland for conducting illegal medical experiments in the Nazi prison camps.

AT THIS POINT, WHAT DIFFERENCE DOES IT MAKE?

Scientists used to be independent individuals, most of whom did not have a degree or a doctorate. Nikola Tesla was probably the greatest scientist in history and he dropped out of university. Michael Faraday, the father of electromagnetic induction, had little formal education.

Today a scientist is someone who can regurgitate the information with which he has been programmed and write papers full of opinions he knows his peers will agree with. To diverge from the consensus is certain professional suicide.

There is nothing wrong with scientific enquiry; the problem comes when it is regarded as a 'priesthood' and run as a cabal.

I have given you these examples in the hope that it might dent your faith in the consensus. Scientists are only human, they have to eat. They will follow the money. If the government or big business offers funding to find evidence of something, you can bet your shoes that they will find a queue of scientists willing to do the work.

MATERIALISTIC WORLDVIEW

Unfortunately, the combination of an increasingly totalitarian and insidious form of world government, and a scientific priesthood, entirely dependent on maintaining the status quo, has created a perfect storm that has effectively turned the 'establishment' against its own people.

The weapon used to control the people was philosophical materialism.

Philosophical materialism began in Greece over two and a half thousand years ago, but it metastasised in the nineteenth century into a far more virulent and dangerous animal known as 'Cultural Marxism'.

Prior to the First World War, Communist intellectuals believed that the workers of the world would rise up and take control of the their own countries, if they only had the chance.

Marxist terrorists in Germany created the 'Frankfurt School'. They mixed the ideas of Marx with those of the psychiatrist Sigmund Freud and created a subversive system to destroy Western culture from within. Being essentially cowards, in 1934 they moved the Frankfurt School to Columbia University in America to get away from the Nazis (7).

After the Second World War, it was obvious that people were just not interested in revolution and subversion. So the Frankfurt School concentrated on the subversion of society through the education system. The 1960s saw the fruition of this ingenious plan.

To Marx and to Stalin, human life was entirely material and therefore expendable. This is a view shared by the Cultural Marxism of today.

The stated aims of Cultural Marxism are as follows:

- *Destroy the family*
- *Destroy any sense of right and wrong*
- *Make sex a tool to destroy society*
- *Destroy a people's pride in their own culture*
- *Destroy a people's belief in their own country*
- *Create violent divisions between groups within a country*
- *Enforce group-think rather than individual enquiry*

If the nation can be destroyed, it is easy to manipulate the people. It is for this reason that the European Project seeks to destroy nations, while at the same time, encouraging divisions both real and imagined between groups of people.

Over the last fifty years all world governments have shifted heavily to the left just as history was proving how dangerous Marxism was. As Marxism died under the weight of its own stupidity, governments around the world decided that the one thing we all needed more of was Marxism.

This would indicate that Cultural Marxism has been incredibly effective in taking control of the masses.

Irrespective of your political beliefs, these are historical facts. At the moment, it is irrelevant if we view socialism as a good or a bad thing. The effects on our day-to-day life are evident. Governments and countries rise and fall. They don't concern me here. All I care about is your happiness and your spiritual freedom.

Mostly we have been trained not to see these ideas as corrosive and we have been programmed not to question their validity, but if you want to wake up and take control of your life, it is vital to question these ideas. We must be prepared to challenge the very bedrock of our modern worldview.

DARWIN THE DROPOUT

The man responsible for our loss of hope was Charles Darwin.

According to his biography, Charles Robert Darwin, as a young man, was considered by everyone who knew him to be somewhat 'thick'. He flunked medical school, he ditched divinity school but he had a rich family and that's all Chucky really needed.

He also happened to come up with the one story the world wanted to hear at exactly the right time. He published *'The Origin of Species by Means of Natural Selection'* in 1859.

For two thousand years, the church had been abusing its power. It was natural that the people would welcome anything, no matter how ridiculous, that would weaken the grip of the church.

Darwin speculated that entirely accidental mutations occur in all life forms. He reasoned that some of those accidental mutations might be useful and provide a competitive advantage to survival. Those mutations, through natural selection, would therefore be passed on through the process of reproduction.

Darwinian theory *assumes* that life began by accident, although he didn't explicitly say so in his book. However, in his personal correspondence he encouraged others to pull the trigger on the gun he lacked the guts to fire.

That's it! That is Darwinian Evolution, I kid you not! I didn't make it up!

Obviously Chucky had never grown up with animals! He had no understanding of animal behaviour. In my experience, animals in the wild kill mutations at birth. So the whole theory falls flat right there.

When I'm really depressed, I cheer myself up by trying to imagine the dinosaur, that couldn't feed himself, trying to explain to his mother that he was trying to turn into a bird. If that wasn't bad enough can you imagine how hard it would have been for him to find a mate?

"He's a what?" the prospective father-in-law would shout! "I don't care if he identifies as a bird! You are a dinosaur and you're not marrying a dinosaur that thinks he's a bird! And what's a bird anyway!"

The deeper you dig into Darwinian theory the sillier it gets.

Dr David Berlinski states that the fossil record doesn't support evolutionary theory or any theory.

He explains that if Darwin was right then we should see more interspecies plasticity in the laboratory, but we don't (8).

Every example given to support Darwin's dream has proven to be false (9).

- *Whales:* No! Always whales - that bit that they tell you were 'back legs' the whale actually needs to have sex. Ambulocetus was a kind of crocodile. Rodhocetus had hands and not fins and it didn't have the tail that Dr Phil Gingerich at first imagined and (helpfully) drew in. Despite the fact Rodhocetus has been proven to be a fake, it is still in the textbooks! Why?

- *Archaeopteryx:* No! Always a bird - nothing like a dinosaur. Proper birds found earlier.

- *Piltdown Man:* No! Fake - Charles Dawson painted an orangutan jaw to look old and put it with a 50,000 year old skull.

Arthur Smith Woodward, keeper of the department of Geology at the British museum didn't notice the hoax, which says a lot about consensus scientists and their objectivity. This fraud was taught as a fact for thirty years. Despite the fact that this was an obvious fake, it's still in textbooks.

- *Haeckel's Embryos:* No! Fake - Professor (another scientist) Ernst Haeckel, was a fine artist and a great supporter of Darwin. He made a series of drawings showing how embryos share a biological evolution. He used his imagination to make reality fit his theory. He was not the last scientist to do that. Again versions of this fraud are still to be found in textbooks!

- *Nebraska Man:* No! Fake - In 1922 Harold Cook found a tooth and said that it was evidence of a prehistoric man. The top scientific 'experts' used this tooth to win the Scopes trial in Dayton, Tennessee in 1925. They scoffed at anyone who would dare to question the opinion of 'scientists'. As it turned out Nebraska man was a pig!

- *Java Man:* No! Wishful thinking - only a tooth, a skullcap and a thighbone found but unlikely to be from the same individual. It was deduced that he walked upright from the thighbone. Age of layer where bones found unknown. According to Dr Hrdlicka "None of the published illustrations or the casts now in various institutions are accurate. Especially is this true of the teeth and the thighbone. The new brain cast is very close to human. The femur is without question human." Science New Series, Vol. 58, Aug 17 1923.

- *Neanderthal Man:* No! Different kind of human with rickets - Professor Reiner Protsch Von Sietan, at Frankfurt University, has been systematically lying about the ages of 'Neanderthal man' for the last thirty years. He dated a female skeleton to 21,300 years, and another skull to 27,400 years old. (In reality 3,300 and 260 years respectively!) Basically they were just different kinds of human just as Australian aboriginal people are different to Northern Europeans but still human. Most of us carry about 2% Neanderthal DNA.

- *Lucy the hominid:* No! Extinct form of ape - parts of the skeleton are actually from a baboon. Head similar to a gorilla. Investigator Richard Leakey concluded that the skeleton is made up of at least three species. Pelvis reconstructed from 40 parts to look humanoid. In museums usually displayed with human feet but skeleton did not include feet? Only 1.1 metre tall and lived in trees.

- *Tktaalik:* No! Wishful thinking - Fins not connected to main skeleton so could not support weight. Too early, evolutionary dead end. The Nunavut Field Project was specifically launched to find the predicted intermediate form. Fish existed prior to 500 million years ago. Tetrapods existed 365 million years ago. Tktaalik was lauded as the transition between fish and Tetrapods at 375 million years. Problem: another Tktaalik found at 390 million years. Not a transitional species but a different extinct species, which remained stable for 25 million years until extinction.

- *Eohippus (little horse):* No! Fake! - O. C. Marsh created Eohippus from fossils scattered all over the world. Modern horses found in strata lower than Eohippus. All fossils that have been offered as examples of transitional species have been found from the same time period. No evidence of any transition in teeth type.

- *Peppered Moth:* No! Micro-evolution at best.

- *Pod Mrcaru Lizards:* (I'll let you make up your own mind!) In 1971, biologists (as an experiment to find evidence for evolutionary adaptation) took five pairs of Italian Wall Lizards from their home on the tiny island of Pod Kopiste, which is quite isolated and away from the main island. They put them on an island next to the main island called Pod Mrcaru. Obviously they had no idea about the native population of lizards on Pod Mrcaru at the time. Neither did they isolate any lizards as a control group. Not long after this, the Croatian/Bosnian war kicked off and the project was abandoned. In 2004, tourism to the islands recommenced. The biologists returned in 2004, 2005 and 2006. Abracadabra! They found different lizards! So they obviously concluded that their five pairs of Italian Wall Lizards must have evolved. Obviously, from a scientific point of view, you have a group of scientists who are being paid to find evidence of evolution, they take five pairs of lizards into an environment that they couldn't possibly ensure was sterile. After 36 years and a war, they return and find different lizards? Colour me surprised! They assure us that the DNA is the same but that only proves that the lizards are still lizards? This is the stick with which Dawkins beats creationists! Really! What is the difference between a blind belief in the Pod Mrcaru Lizards and a belief in the relics of saints?

- *Coelacanths: Evidence against* - Fossils of this large fish found that indicate it is over 350 million years old — The BBC have reported that over 300 live specimens have been found in Asia. No sign of any evolution. They've stayed exactly the same for 350 million years.

- *Damselfly: Evidence against* - Fossils over 300 million years old. Thriving community of living Damselflies in south-western Australia. No sign of any evolutionary mutations.

As Dr Berlinski says, *"dogs stay dogs, bugs stay bugs."*

"Random variation, natural selection, is not sufficient to account for the level of complexity we see around us."
  Dr Berlinski

It's quite a thing when we need Eddie Griffin, my favourite comedian, to talk sense about evolution, "If we evolved from monkeys in Africa, how come there are still monkeys in Africa? Are they the retarded monkeys?"

Richard Dawkins, himself, does a bit of stand-up comedy trying to explain this obvious anomaly. He points to a picture of a white secretary from Stoke-on-Trent and assures us that she descended, along with chimps and gorillas, from a common ancestor. He offers no evidence but because he's white, and has a soothing Oxford accent, people believe him.

This is a religious belief just the same as the belief that the world is only five thousand years old and was covered in a worldwide flood.

All fossils are of complete animals. We have never seen a 'work in progress' with odd bits of mutation.

WHY IS THIS IMPORTANT?

Without Darwin there would have been no way for philosophical materialism to become the dominant worldview.

It may be for that reason that the establishment has put so much money into propping up the theory and is so ready to falsify the evidence. It may also be the reason that texts books still regularly include evidences that have been proven to be false. Philosophical materialism is a religion.

Due to Darwin's theory of evolution and the rise of philosophical materialism, we are programmed to believe that living beings are just machines.

HOW DARWIN ACCIDENTALLY GAVE BIRTH TO HITLER

In such a barren and meaningless world, it was perfectly logical for the tobacco companies to brainwash the entire world into smoking their deadly cigarettes. Darwin's cousin, Francis Galton advocated the killing of unfit races (black people) and created the movement we now call *Eugenics.*

Eugenics took root in America and gave rise to forced sterilisations and population control. Funded by the Carnegie Institution and the Rockefeller Foundation to name but two.

In 1906, J. H. Kellogg (yes! your breakfast cereal) provided funding to help found the Race Betterment Foundation. Naturally the scientists followed the money!

Margaret Sanger advocated *sterilisation for Negroes* or anyone she thought was 'feeble minded'. She went on to found the *'Planned Parenthood'* network (10).

Hitler was so impressed with American eugenics and Carnegie Institute's system of euthanasia and sterilisation that he encouraged German doctors to study in America at the Euthanasia Society of America. Indeed many Nazi Eugenicist Doctors were spared execution at the end of the war and were quickly taken to the US.

I'm not sure what any of the Marlboro Man cowboys would have thought about eugenics but as they all died of smoking-related diseases; I can hazard a good guess!

DON'T BE INTIMIDATED

It has become fashionable to dismiss any divergence from the consensus opinion by saying, 'I believe in science'.

Don't be put off; science isn't something you can 'believe' in! It is a method of enquiry. The process of science is to observe phenomena, formulate hypothesis regarding it and test to see if the hypothesis is true.

If you say you 'believe' then you have already excluded yourself from the scientific process due to your own preconceived ideas. The next tactic is to attack the questioner or to dismiss the question. This again is not science. Science is not 'done' through consensus, it is not democratic. 'Science' is based on logic and evidence.

Always examine primary evidence and above all trust your own common sense. If you think it sounds phoney then there is a good chance it is!

YOU CAN'T READ A BOOK IN THE DARK

If I could give you a book that explained the secrets of the universe, it would be useless to you if you couldn't read it! You might make a collection of books from other teachers, philosophers and mystics but none of them would be able to help you and for the same reason. If you live in the dark, you cannot possibly read our words.

From the moment that we are born, we form our worldview out of the stories we hear. In ways so subtle that we don't even notice the process, we are programmed to look at life in a particular way.

The 'Darkness' that we live in is a very specific worldview that convinces us not to trust our own power. If 'natural selection' created us then love is, obviously, an enemy to our survival. If life is an accident then we are truly condemned to live alone in a pointless world.

This corrosive worldview has infected every aspect of our lives so deeply that we hardly notice the rot anymore. Darwin and philosophical materialism have taken human civilisation back to the Stone Age.

It is true that human history is full of stories of war, cruelty and stupidity but what has proved so corrosive to Western civilisation is the 'normalising' of the idea that life is entirely accidental and devoid of any meaning. In this way, the world is left in a moral desert with a compass that invariably points us in the wrong direction.

The entire arc of this book is focussed on the search for a logical, coherent and scientific explanation for the world our senses detect but to which our materialist worldview has kept us entirely blind.

ISTANBUL/CONSTANTINOPLE

The door hissed back and revealed the plastic corridor leading into the Istanbul terminal. Already the aisle was jammed with small men with frightening moustaches fighting to be the first off the plane. Eventually Vin Diesel with the hat waded into them and some kind of order was restored.

It was obvious that the Turkish architect used in Baku must have been busy elsewhere when they made the airport at Istanbul. There was something 'disposable' about it. I had to check-in for my connection so I ran for the desk. I should have checked my facts before I committed so much energy!

There never was a plane allocated to my slot! The girl at the Information desk shrugged in a way that suggested, *'What do you expect!'*

It looked like a long wait and a stack of missed connections, but before I got on the phone to my agent I thought it would be a good idea to get fed.

★★★★

CHAPTER 4

THE 'SELF OF 'NOW'

Like an egg and spoon race, I'd managed to successfully balance an open bottle of beer, a cheese croissant and an espresso on a white plastic tray while sprinting for the last empty table. Some Italians were kind enough to give me a small round of applause of appreciation for my demonstration. I gave them a nod by way of a bow, as I squeezed myself into the flimsy plastic chair.

By the time that I noticed the large man in a chicken suit it was too late. I was in the middle of air travel's worst nightmare, the stag party.

To my left, there were a group of men who could only be described as legless. Most of them were wearing pyjamas but it was the man in the chicken suit that worried me most. He was red.

He was too drunk to take the suit off and it was obvious that if he didn't pull the hood down soon, he was going to pass out. The Italians were already taking bets on how long he would remain conscious.

Air travel used to be magical; we used to look forward to it. I'm not sure when I started dreading it!

It's true that the threat of terrorism has made air travel more inconvenient, but there are few things that terrify the seasoned traveller more that the British stag party.

For some reason, perfectly ordinary young men think that it's really funny to dress up, get drunk and be as loud and as obnoxious as possible. It usually involves heartfelt intimate conversations conducted in public at the top of their voice.

I usually try to make it a habit to get re-seated before the projectile vomiting begins.

Today I was not so lucky. Mr Chicken Suit erupted over the table and fell to the floor. The Italians were delighted.

Once upon a time, the oil that lubricated the machine of Western civilisation was good manners. Good manners are the expression of a concern for the well-being of others. My mother taught me that having good table manners ensures that people remember you for your conversation and not for the mess you make of the soup. How did society become so ugly so quickly?

A part of that answer is obviously the rise of the materialist 'self-centred' worldview but that begs the question, 'If the self is at the centre of our world, where and what is this self'?

WHAT IS THE SELF?

If I asked you to point to the part of your body where your 'self' lives, which part would you point to?

So is your 'self' in your brain? It has been shown that a human being can lose 95% of his brain and still have an IQ of 126 and a degree in mathematics (1). So if your 'self' is not in your brain, where is it?

It used to be said that the 'self' lived in the heart but we change those out every day. Just because you get a new heart, it doesn't make you a new person.

Your arms and legs then? No! Sadly, people lose them every day and don't lose themselves.

What about your memories? Scientists have not been able to find memories in the brain and people lose their memories for various reasons but they are still essentially the same person (2).

A few decades and many millions of dollars ago, scientists promised us that they would find the 'self' in our DNA but that has proved to be a dead end. As it turns out DNA are just the building blocks of life. DNA does not contain the plan or the builder (3).

So where exactly is the 'self'? If you close your eyes and keep very quiet, you will observe some thoughts go past the window of your mind. Beneath those thoughts you will find emotions. Is that where the real 'you' lives?

In order to move forward with this investigation, let's do a thought experiment.

IMAGINE THIS SCENARIO (A):

You are supposed to go on a date with the most desirable person you can imagine. A limousine picks you up to take you to a quiet French restaurant where you have a private room booked. As you approach the room where you are to meet this person, you are told that you must be blindfolded.

As you are led into this room you feel a warm soft, slightly moist, touch on your cheek. Given the logic of the situation you imagine it to be a kiss. Your heart explodes with joy as your knees go weak with desire.

Now imagine a slightly different scenario that involves exactly the same physical stimulus:

IMAGINE THIS SCENARIO (B):

The world has ended. The undead have taken over the world. You are starving. Armed with only an old flashlight and a plastic spork you have to descend into the cellar of an old building to find something to eat. You can hear the drip-drip of water and the echo as your foot crunches on the granite step. Near the bottom of the staircase you can see cobwebs and empty boxes. Your flashlight fails. You are frozen in fear. Something warm and slightly moist touches your cheek! What do you think your reaction would be?

In both of these scenarios the physical stimulus was the same: darkness and a warm, moist touch on your cheek. The only things that changed were our belief about the past and our expectation for the future.

It is evident then that our reactions are dependent not so much upon actual events but rather they are based on our beliefs and those beliefs are based on the sum of our past, how we feel about that past and our expectation for the future.

WHY THE SELF OF NOW?

These are the three bricks with which we build our 'Self of Now'.

- *The sum of our past*

- *How we feel about that past*

- *Our expectations for our future*

This idea of the 'Self of Now' has no inherent or independent reality. Change any one of those three things and your 'idea' of self will change.

The more we focus our mind and the power of our intention inward toward our core, it is as though a cloud begins to form within a cloudless sky.

This cloud slowly coagulates under the massive centripetal force of our intention into something almost solid.

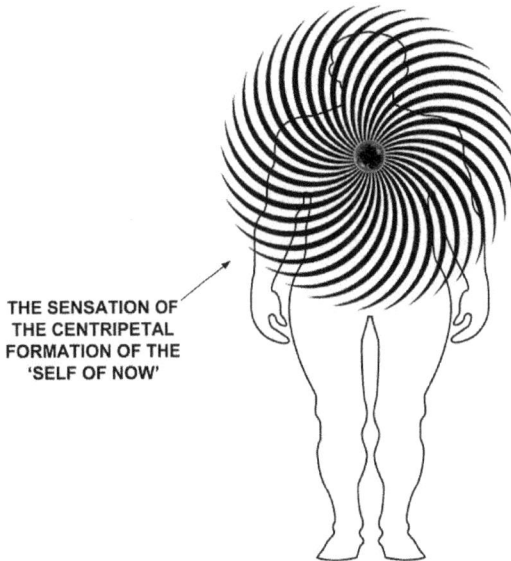

THE SENSATION OF THE CENTRIPETAL FORMATION OF THE 'SELF OF NOW'

[Image 1: Centripetal formation of the 'Self of Now'.]

I use the term 'Self of Now' because this aspect of ourselves doesn't care about us. The 'Self of Now' doesn't care about the you in five minutes or the you of tomorrow. Your 'Self of Now' will always push you toward things that will satisfy it at the expense of everything you hold dear.

The extra cake, the next bottle of wine, the affair with the secretary, why is it that our addictions always seem to destroy us?

Don't believe me? Let's look at some examples.

GREED:

Close your eyes and remember a time when you were carrying some plates of food to the table. Maybe you are carrying some cake! Maybe you are bringing cake for your children, your husband, maybe someone you love.

You glance down and realise that one plate has more or maybe it has something on it that you really want. It's your favourite.

Do you remember that split second when you felt the urge to take the best plate for yourself?

Where did that urge come from? Would you take the food out of your loved one's mouth? Is that really the kind of person you are?

ANGER:

Can you remember a time when you were really busy or stressed and someone needed your help? Maybe it was your children, maybe your dog, maybe someone at work?

Just for that second you felt the flash of anger. Maybe you did actually snap at little Johnny. Can you remember the hurt look on his face?

Did you kick the dog or did you throw something at the cat?

Is that anger really who you are? Where did it come from?

ANXIETY:

To further clarify the arising of the 'Self of Now'. Let's look at how we deal with being in crowds.

It's true that not many of us like to be in big crowds. Most of us get nervous and our behaviour changes.

In scenario A - we arrive at the check-in and there has been a computer glitch. The concourse is packed with people. We begin to feel the urge to panic. We want to run, our vision narrows. We become clumsy because we are shutting down our external sensors. We become agitated and aggressive. We react with anger if someone pushes in front of us.

In this scenario we are seeing the world entirely through our idea of the 'Self of Now'. This creates a centripetal tension. This direction of intention further solidifies our sense of self and separation from the universe. Just as an apple falls when we drop it, so too is suffering the inevitable product when we direct our intention toward the 'Self of Now'.

Now let's look at scenario B - As you approach the airport arrivals concourse it is packed with the same people as in scenario A but only this time I give you a glimpse of everyone of your past lives since time began. In that split second of transcendental clarity you realise that every one of those people in the concourse had at sometime loved you and cared for you.

Can you imagine the urge to wave to the crowd and the feeling of belonging. You would want to touch the hands of all the people there.

In scenario B you would feel pleasure but in scenario A you would feel stress. Only the nature of the three bricks changed: the story of your past, how you feel about that past and your expectations for your future.

Unfortunately, most of us for most of the time become entirely hijacked by the flow of our thoughts and emotions to the point that we live our lives unconscious of the world around us. In many ways we live our lives like Zombies entirely controlled by the 'Self of Now'.

HIJACKED BY THE SELF OF NOW

I've taken the day off and it's a lovely spring afternoon. My thoughts emerge out of my emotions and float past my mind like twigs floating on the river.

As I cast my rod into the shade of a willow tree, I feel hungry. My mind follows the thought and I wonder what my wife packed for lunch.

Following that thought, I wonder what's for supper tonight. I remember that my wife said that she had a vegetable curry in the freezer. I follow that thought as it flows past the thought of the vegetable curry. In my mind I am a long way now from the river where I'm standing. In seconds my mind has been hijacked by my 'random' thoughts. I'm existing now entirely in the 'Self of Now'.

It occurs to me that the freezer is not working properly and it seems to be using a lot of electricity. It then occurs to me that our quarterly electricity bill is due and my pay check is going to be late. My stomach lurches with fear. I bite my lip.

From my fear, I begin to feel anger. I remember that my wife is shopping in the city with her mother today. I remember thinking that she is spending too much money on the children. I make a mental note to ask the bank for an overdraft.

At that moment, my mobile phone vibrates in my pocket. I answer my phone and it's my wife who is really excited. She has managed to find a rare book on fly-fishing that I've wanted for years. She can hardly contain her happiness as she tells me that she got the book for five hundred dollars.

"You paid how much?" I scream down the phone. The line goes quiet.

"Take the bloody thing back", I shout at the phone as I hold it in front of my face like a deadly snake I'd just caught in a mid-air attack.

"But it was for your birthday!" I hear my wife say through her tears.

"Why are you in such a bad mood? You're out fishing! You should be happy!"

I don't know what to say? I feel terrible for making my wife cry and I don't know how we got from fishing to a big row about money but I can't back down now. I hang up the phone and just about stop myself from throwing it at the willow tree.

You probably recognise something of yourself in those examples. Most of us are the victims of our own automatic reactions. We just shake our head and put it down to a moment of insanity.

We apologise eventually, but the truth is you can never unsay what has been said. You can never undo what has been done.

THE BLACK WOLF

It is important to recognise that the 'Self of Now', the source of those thoughts, seems to have its own agenda. It behaves as if it was an individual in its own right.

Throughout history, different cultures have come up with stories and legends to account for the unpredictability and apparent independence of our automatic thoughts.

There is a Native American legend that explains that when we are born into this world we have two spirit guides, the Black Wolf and the White Wolf.

The Black Wolf is the 'Self of Now'. Born into a body limited by our five senses, the Black Wolf believes that he is alone in this strange and hostile world. He has been driven mad by the isolation of his prison. Just as a wolf will bite his own foot off in order to escape a trap, the Black Wolf seeks to consume the world in order to be free of it.

The White Wolf is the 'Self of Tomorrow' but the wolf we live with is the one we feed.

Obviously, I'm not saying that there really are animal spirit guides living inside of us. I include the legend only to demonstrate that the 'Self of Now' is not a new idea.

WHY ARE ADDICTIONS ALWAYS SELF-DESTRUCTIVE

Have you ever had that drink too many? Have you had that cigarette, that cake, that hit, that affair that destroyed your marriage?

Why is it that our greed, our addictions, only satisfy the 'Self of Now' and inevitably betrays the 'Self of Tomorrow'?

Why is it that our automatic reactions are so rarely a force of good in our lives?

Have you ever woken up to the evidence of your own stupidity and said to yourself, 'I don't believe I did that!' Have you ever looked around for someone else to blame? Why does the 'Self of Now' always ruin our life?

In the face of our own addictions we can't help but feel 'out of control'. Who is in charge? Why would we sabotage ourselves? Why do the urges, that push us toward immediate gratification, go against our long-term goals and ideals? In fact, why do they usually destroy everything we love and hold dear?

In 2011, Alexander Rhodes founded the 'NoFap' movement for men, after a 2003 Chinese study demonstrated that if men can avoid masturbation for seven days they can boost their testosterone by 45%. Once Alexander looked into how dangerous the masturbation habit was in men, he became something of an evangelical advocate for the NoFap movement.

Unfortunately, for men, masturbation and the use of porn is an addictive habit. It is a great metaphor for the way the 'Self of Now' will betray the 'Self of Tomorrow' in a habit that is inherently self-destructive.

Centuries of repression were stripped away in the 1960s and young men were encouraged by the establishment to fap themselves stupid and we did. Unfortunately, apart from the negative physical consequences, the social and psychological damage of this solitary addiction are beyond the scope of this book to list.

Our addictions are as varied as humans are inventive, but the one thing they all have in common is the fact that eventually all of them ruin your life.

There is an old Jewish saying, 'We cling to the demons as they destroy us'.

An entire industry has been created just to sell people more 'self' but is that really what they need?

We have seen from the above examples that most people don't even understand what the 'self' is?

I'M OFFENDED!

The 'Self of Now' will build a fence around you and will tell you that you 'HATE' everything outside of it. You don't like Republicans, you definitely hate Trump and you only like Vegans. Someone else will decide that they hate Blacks, Muslims and Jews.

It is in this way that the 'Self of Now' will destroy us all, if we let it.

If you feel the need to shut people up before they can even explain their ideas, there's a good chance it's not really you! It's just the 'Self of Now' trying to stop you ever finding out that you are being controlled.

The new fashion for street protests is a great example of this. We chant mindless and childish rhymes and glory in being in a group of people who all have the same opinions as we do. This isn't political action it's self-approbation.

Destruction of the 'other' is heroin to the 'Self of Now'. You only have to look at the faces of these people, as they shout their chants, they all have the same look of mindless ecstasy.

A GENIE IN A BOTTLE

Because the 'Self of Now' is fundamentally an illusion it cannot really provide happiness, or long-term fulfilment, in your life. Like some malevolent Arabian Jinn the 'Self of Now' promises to grant us our darkest wish but just as in Arab Folklore, the Jinn is always a liar. Whatever we wish for will result in our destruction.

We are always eventually destroyed by our own greed and our willingness to believe in the genie's promises.

Harvey Weinstein's 'Self of Now' told him that he could have any woman he wanted. We all know how that ended!

The 'Self of Now' is extremely limited in its view. It can only see two roads ahead, the external and internal route to happiness. As we have already discussed, both of those formulas have been proven to not work. Neither adding things to yourself nor changing things about your self will give you peace.

WILL THE REAL 'ME' PLEASE STAND UP!

Your happiness and your ability to deal with the problems in your life depend on you gaining the ability to notice where your urges, emotions and thoughts come from.

But don't worry! There is a real you that exists underneath your 'idea' of you, beneath your 'Self of Now'.

Think about it! If you can 'observe' your thoughts, emotions and urges, who is doing the 'observing'?

The 'Self of Now' is an illusion! It is just the reflection of the accidents of our lives.

The QM4YS system will teach you how to be mindful of your inner life and experience directly the arising of the 'Self of Now'.

It's not easy! It takes work, practice, failure and then more practice but everyone can do it! All you have to do is really want to.

FLIGHT DELAYED

I'd just managed to get Mr Chicken Suit into the recovery position and removed his hood, when one of his friends made a lunge for me. As it turned out, the man who was trying to kiss me was a Police Detective Inspector from Liverpool.

Dave, the man in the chicken suit, was a sergeant.

By the time the Turkish Police arrived, most of the Liverpool Police stag party had sobered up and were beginning to regret wearing pyjamas without underpants.

With visions of the film 'Midnight Run' in my head, I beat a hasty retreat and made my way to find a departures board.

CHAPTER 5

****

BENEATH THE WHITE NOISE

My Air France connection to Düsseldorf had been delayed yet again and I was on my two hundredth circuit of the shopping mall. In an effort to avoid a young man who was trying to sell me a raffle ticket for a car I could never afford to insure, I sidestepped into a music shop.

A sales girl looked up hopefully but I managed to avoid eye contact. I could see the car salesman, circling like an angry shark, outside the shop door. I made my way to the back of the shop, hopping he would lose my scent. After having been forcibly perfumed by sales girls on circuit 51, 123 and 154, I glumly mused that he would be able to track my sickly scent all the way back to London.

A pair of headphones with earpieces like pillows were cradled above a picture of Wolfgang Amadeus Mozart. The CD on sale was of his unfinished Requiem in D Minor, recorded during a Leonard Bernstein concert. I glanced toward the door only to accidentally catch the eye of my pursuer. He lifted his hand to wave.

I quickly turned and put the headphones on and hit play. I was immediately hit by a wall of sound that made me temporarily disorientated. In shock, I pulled the headphones off and looked for a volume control.

The music shop sales girl was watching me like a hawk. She reached for the phone like she was considering calling for security. I put my briefcase down and pulled the headphones back on.

MOZART AND YOUR INNER LIFE:
Mozart hit me like a wall of sound. The headphones were remarkable. The sound wrapped around me like a caress.

When you first listen to this kind of music it seems like an incoherent wall of sound. It feels like a huge wave that rolls over you. In the same way our own inner life washes over us and carries us to places we never planned to go. If you listen very carefully you will begin to make out individual voices and instruments.

I remember my favourite niece once told me that she had been to a party in Tokyo with Leonard Bernstein and he had explained to her that, as a conductor, within a concert full of dozens of musicians and singers he could hear one dud note played by one single player.

Similarly, if we are to gain control over the 'Self of Now', and indeed our lives, we have to learn to listen to our inner life with that kind of concentration. We have to be able to hear the beginning of every ugly note in our mind. Because it is these ugly notes deep within our emotions and thoughts that create the suffering in our lives.

GAINING CONTROL OVER THE SELF OF NOW

Just as it is impossible to learn to swim without getting in the water, so too is it impossible to take control of your life without practice and effort. There is no new information or realisation that will provide you with control over the 'Self of Now'.

It is for this reason that mental training and self-awareness is a fundamental part of the QM4YS system.

If you are anything like me, and 99% of my students, at this point your 'Self of Now' will be whining like a spoilt five-year-old child, *'I haven't got time!' 'I will never be able to silence my mind!' 'I can't concentrate on anything!'*.

Congratulations! The more your 'Self of Now' tries to sabotage your efforts, the more you can have confidence that you are heading in the right direction.

Think for a moment, of course you can concentrate! Do you watch television, or go to the movies? Do you listen to music, or have conversations with friends? Maybe you play some form of sport.

Anytime that you become totally absorbed by something, you are concentrating 100%. You can concentrate that hard simply because the 'Self of Now' allows you to!

The QM4YS system gives you the tools you need to take back control of your own inner life from the 'Self of Now'.

With regard to having enough time to sit and train: it only takes ten minutes a day to turn your life around. Imagine that you've eaten something that didn't agree with you. Are you telling me that you wouldn't find an extra ten minutes a day to sit on the loo? If you can find ten minutes a day to go the toilet, I am sure you can find ten minutes a day to repair your life! The rewards are more than worth the effort.

For instance, I was born the last child into a family that had already been destroyed by its own casual evil. My sisters hated me with a passion. My eldest sister tried, several times, to have me killed.

Over the years I developed a Pavlovian response to their voices. Once upon a time, I only had to hear someone with a similar accent to my sisters for me to want to beat them to death with a baseball bat. Obviously, the direction of my intention only allowed me to see the world through my 'idea' of myself.

Eventually, I learnt to be able to go beneath my thoughts and emotions.

When I eventually managed to change the direction of my intention outward and resist the Automatic Negative Thoughts, slowly my hate dissolved into a terrible grief at the loss of the sisters whom I now realised I loved so much. In the end, I realised that my capacity for hate was in direct proportion to my capacity for profound love.

In fact, my love for my sisters was the only thing that was real.

If I didn't love them so much they would never have been able to hurt me. Their hatred for 'me' was just their own fantasy; one that they couldn't escape from because they were lost within their own 'Self of Now'.

Without acquiring the ability to clearly resolve our inner symphony into separate sounds, we are forever condemned to be the slave of the accidents of our lives.

For anyone in the modern world who wants to take up some kind of mental discipline, the danger is that there are so many different people out there trying to sell them books and courses. The problem is that all of those courses almost exclusively deal with the 'Self of Now'. There are many choices but only one real option.

ANY COLOUR YOU LIKE AS LONG AS IT'S BLACK:
Noticing that the car salesmen had left, I sneaked out of the music shop. Quickly forgetting my narrow escape, I returned to window shopping.

Have you ever noticed how the shop names may change but the clothes all look the same? There must be a clothes factory in Sri Lanka that is forever stuck in 1968 California.

You can pass shops with signs that say BOSS, Calvin Klein, Gant, River Island and they're all determined to sell you clothes that would only be appropriate if you were a young man in the California of John. F. Kennedy.

It's as though we are forever stuck in some kind of hellish time loop of warm beer and pretzels.

When I was young enough to wear those clothes, Hugo Boss had not long ago transformed itself from designing the uniforms for the Nazi Party. Armani made his name by recreating 1940s Italian style for overweight American businessmen of the 80s. We didn't have much money then but we had lots of choice.

Now it seems that the more shops there are, and the more money I have, the less choice I have. You can have any nametag you want as long as it comes from that one factory in Sri Lanka and 1968 California.

Similarly, in the world of today, if you want to do something about the suffering in your life, you have many options but **only one choice**.

THE SECRET OF CAR REPAIR

As we've already discussed, the airport bookshops are full of paperbacks selling self-help books of one sort or another. You can buy CDs of Guided Meditations, or Eckhart's ever present stuff on 'mindfulness'. You might pick up a book on various organised religions. You could even go to the chemist and fulfil your prescription for anti-depressants.

The problem is none of these systems work and for the same reason: they deal with the symptom of your suffering and not the disease. They concentrate entirely on the 'Self of Now'.

In order to explain let me give you an analogy, imagine that you'd won the raffle for the Aston Martin DB9. As you might expect, it has broken down yet again and you are stuck on the side of the road. Obviously you couldn't afford roadside assistance so in the language of the Bard, 'You are royally stuffed!'

Your choices at this point are as follows:

- *Guided Meditation:* Put your wonderful leather seat into recline and play some music on the impressive Bose speakers. Make yourself feel better in the short-term and ignore the fundamental problem at hand. This is exactly the same as using any of the plethora of 'Guided Mediations' on offer. As guided meditation is actually a form of hypnosis it only really engages your emotions and changes your thoughts in the short-term.

- *Mindfulness Meditation:* You could pop the hood and look at the marvel that is engineering at Aston Martin. You could watch the engine at it runs but as you are not a mechanic nor do you have access to the diagnostic computer required, you are simply the watching the engine run while it is broken. This is, in my opinion, the same as using 'Eckhart Tolle's' version of Beat-Zen. I studied Soto Zen Buddhism for thirty-five years and after studying at many centres and monasteries around the world, I can confirm that, on its own, meditation is useless. Mindfulness, on its own, is just like watching a broken engine run.

- *Drugs:* You may decide to use your spare time in painting a 'go-faster' stripe down the side of your newly acquired DB9. You could even get a container of rocket fuel from the boot and siphon it into the tank. You could add those fantastic suspension systems so beloved by Mexican Drug Cartels. This is the same as using drugs to solve the problem of the pain in your life. Given that Dr Peter Breggin, America's leading psychiatrist, has already testified to the Supreme Court that there is no evidence for a chemical imbalance in the brain that causes emotional problems. It follows then that putting toxic substances into your body in the hope that it might do some good is like putting jet fuel in a broken car.

- *Self-Help and Motivational Books:* Stuck as you are on the side of the road, if it starts to rain, you could sit back in the car and read John Steinbeck's 'Travels with Charley' about his journey around America with his French poodle. You could read David Dowsey's wonderful book, 'Aston Martin: Power, Beauty and Soul'. None of this would help you fix your car of course but at least you would feel motivated. Obviously this is exactly like reading most 'self-help' books - like our clothes factory in Sri Lanka - they churn out different versions of the same old design that we have been stuck with for the last forty years.

If I have to read one more book on 'Love yourself', 'Self-Love' or 'Don't give a F##K', I swear I will do time for the author.

- *Organised Religion:* Obviously, if by this time you are still waiting for someone to save your broken DB9, you might decide to give religion a go! You could get out of your car and kneel down by the exquisitely designed wing and pray to the god of Aston Martin. You could mentally or at the top of your voice (although I wouldn't recommend it) make a deal with Aston Martin that if only he will get your car to run you promise to give your first born son to him as a mechanic. You may even promise to go to owners club meetings every Sunday for the rest of your life. Obviously, as socially desirable as this might be; this, like organised religion, is entirely useless when it comes to dealing with human suffering or indeed fixing a broken DB9.

All of these systems deal exclusively with the 'Self of Now'. Remember the formula?

The Guided Meditation engages your emotions and gives you a new 'past'. You can use hypnosis to create new 'expectations' but ultimately you are just tinkering with the symptoms and not the cause.

Just watching the arising thoughts and emotions on their own, is mildly interesting but unless you fundamentally change the direction of your intention it is not going to help you solve the problem of you.

Drugs just destroy your ability to deal with the problems inside or outside of you.

Self-help books and religion only help you create new expectations.

All of these five systems might, in a limited way, work in the short term but they always fail to address the fundamental problem. It is for this reason that people follow these systems in fads and fashions.

If we are to find a way to a holistic solution to the problems of life, we have to go deeper than that.

MENTAL TRAINING IS A RETURN TO YOUR OWN ESSENCE

To give you a practical example of how internal clarity seems to evolve in a cyclic way, let me describe the normal process of using the will to clear the mind.

When you first close your eyes and look within, often your thoughts, emotions, and feelings are just a chaos that you can't make much sense of.

Very soon you will notice your thoughts emerging from somewhere above and behind the emotions. If you resist the urge to follow the thoughts you will be able to watch your emotions float by like clouds.

Behind the clouds there is a sky, a 'feeling' behind your emotions. This underlying feeling is like a prejudice or some kind of mental limp. It is the feeling through which you view the world.

The 'Self of Now' emerges from within your memories of your past and your expectations for the future, so you will find yourself constantly distracted by thoughts and feelings about your past and about your future.

This is like being lost in a fast flowing river; you will be hijacked by your own inner life. In order to free yourself from this process you throw out an anchor.

The essence of your true self is only ever within this moment so when we bring our mind back to this very moment the 'Self of Now' begins to slowly dissolve. This very moment is all that exists.

When you begin to dissolve the 'Self of Now', you create a little space for the real you to appear. You start to become aware of the formation of the 'Self of Now'.

As you follow a selfish thought you will become aware of the 'Self of Now' solidifying within you like a dark cloud.

DO WE REALLY EXIST?

Many people who use 5-MeO-DMT and other psychedelic drugs, or begin serious training in Zen, may eventually have a psychological crisis or a dissociative state.

When you realise that the world around you and all the things you based your life on don't really exist in the way you believed, it can have a traumatic effect on your mental equilibrium.

It hit me while studying in Vietnam and it nearly killed me because Zen had given me no way to deal with it. I wasn't prepared because my practice, like all Buddhist practice, was still focussed on the 'Self of Now'. Like all religions, Buddhism is focussed on the student getting 'himself' out of the world.

The QM4YS system prevents this psychological danger by pointing the student in the opposite direction and that is the key. When we focus the direction of intention outward, understanding comes naturally and without stress.

The 'Self of Now' is not who you really are because only something external to you can be observed by you. Ultimately, the knife cannot cut itself.

THE DANGERS OF TRANSCENDENTAL TOURISM

As you learn to dissolve the illusion of the 'Self of Now' and connect to the universal matrix, it is inevitable that you will experience reality in a different way.

Unfortunately, the materialistic society has made your journey doubly hard and it has done it in two ways. Because most children no longer have any kind of discipline they find it almost impossible to learn to discipline themselves as adults. The other problem is that we all grow up expecting that our desires will be fulfilled immediately.

A lack of both *patience* and *self-discipline* make it almost inevitable that people will shop for transcendental experiences as though they were some kind of computer game. There are several teachers out there that do indeed sell their courses in this way.

It is for this reason that QM4YS is built upon a community and a coherent system. It is this system that gives us a solid base. The 'Self of Now', like a storybook genie, is used to giving you exactly what you ask for, when you ask for it. Because of this dysfunctional relationship, most of the visions and inner experiences people proudly cling on to are just projections of your 'Self of Now'.

My teacher told me that, '*If you see the Buddha you must kill him*'. What that means is that we must let go of our inner experiences and just continue with our training. If you don't do this you can easily fall into having emotional and mental problems.

Within an infinite sea with no concept of direction, time or space, it is extremely easy to get lost if you don't have a teacher and the support of a community.

RETURN TO THE REAL YOU

Many fashionable gurus and meditation masters teach their students that they must let go of themselves and the world. They smile enigmatically and say that we shouldn't allow ourselves to be attached to the people in our lives.

Some of them, like the Buddha, have seen the 'Self of Now' and have concluded that the world isn't real. This is a big mistake. We tend to believe what we want to believe. The Buddha found what the Buddha went looking for! That was not an accident.

The one thing that all of these gurus have missed, and cannot account for, is the undeniable fact that you are alive and so are the people that you love.

It is possible to use the 'Self of Now' to reduce the world down to atoms but the 'X' in the equation, which they ignore, is the fact that we are alive. Because of this omission they cannot solve the equation that life proposes.

The real you that exists beneath your idea of you cannot be observed and can only be experienced by truly connecting to life, not by detaching from it.

In chapters 7 & 8 we will look at the science behind this system of mental training.

DELAYS

Airports are a preview of the fate of the world. I've gone through major airports all over the world and in all of them the shops are exactly the same. You would think that a one-world government would mean limitless choice for the consumer! You would be wrong.

In every airport, all over the world, you find the same half a dozen shops and each of the shops sell the same rubbish. God help you if you are no longer seventeen.

Women's clothing is designed specifically for a certain kind of American working girl. They only come in size 8.

Jewellery is made in a Russian factory with the same tooling they used to make AK-47s.

No wonder that the suicide rate after long-haul flights is so high.

I had another four hours to wait for my connection. I was beginning to think of taking up smoking again in the hope of an early death.

CHAPTER 6

****

THE 'SELF OF TOMORROW'

At heart I am a gypsy! For many years I've lived on boats of one form or another. Living on boats you get used to not having a television. For as long as I can remember, therefore, videos and DVDs have been an important part of my social life.

With yet another flight delay, it was inevitable then that I found myself in the HMV store.

HOLLYWOOD HOLDS THE SECRET TO EVERYTHING.

Looking along the discount DVD aisle, it occurred to me that most Hollywood films are all the same! They presuppose that their audience share a common expectation. The protagonist of the film must go through a journey and evolve as a person!

Films like Scrooge, Ground Hog Day, Family Man, In Bruges, Unforgiven, The Wrestler, Leon, and Focus (to name but a few) all depend on us subconsciously agreeing with a certain spiritual reality.

Invariably, the protagonist goes from position 'A' to position 'B':

- Position A: Self-obsessed, disconnected from the people around them, spiritually empty.
- Position B: Other centred, connected to the people around them, spiritually full, selfless.

The process of redemption, inevitably involves some kind of journey or quest. This difficult journey creates personal change in the protagonist.

This common theme of redemption would not prove so popular unless it reflected a profound reality of which we are all subconsciously aware.

These stories would not be believable unless *we all instinctively know that the 'Self of Now' is not really our friend* and that only through dissolving our sense of self can we find happiness and our authentic self.

We long for position B so much that we look for someone, a guru, a teacher who may already have it in the hope that some of it might rub off on us! The great joke is that position B is the very essence of who and what we are. What we see in those teachers is only a reflection of what is already inside of us.

WHAT IS THE SELF OF TOMORROW?

When you were a child did you ever make sandcastles on the beach? I remember one summer's day, I must have been six or seven, I had built a sandcastle down near the surf, where the sand is nearly solid. It had four towers and one in the centre. A proud American flag stood six inches above the centre tower.

After lunch I ran down the beach to work on my castle only to see my flag poking out of the water. In a herculean effort to save my castle, I began trying to push the sea away from what was at this point just a mound of sand. Whenever I pushed the sea away, I could see the sand. Each time I stopped to rest, the sea came back.

The sand was everywhere that the sea was not.

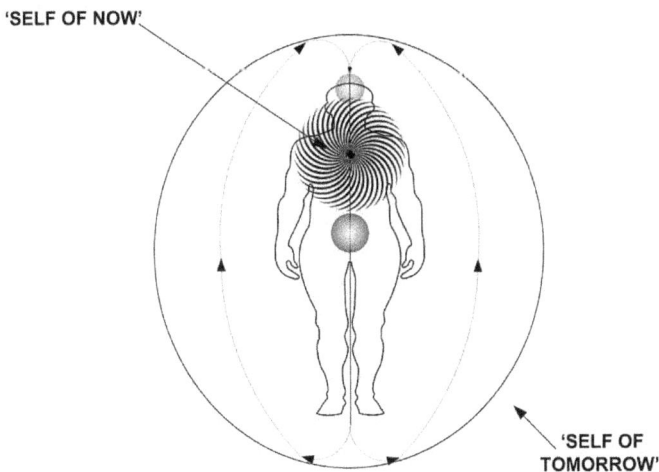

[Image 2: The 'Self of Now' Vs. The 'Self of Tomorrow'.]

Finding the 'Self of Tomorrow' is a lot like that. With great effort we train ourselves to restrict our automatic reactions. We learn to be mindful and to notice the arising of the 'Self of Now' and practice letting that arising go.

When we do that, we can experience the clear lake of our true self but the moment we stop working on our self, the 'Self of Now' floods back like the sea. Inevitably we slowly revert to our old habits of mind.

The truth is that the 'Self of Tomorrow' is everywhere the 'Self of Now' is not.

WHAT IS THE NATURE OF THE SELF OF TOMORROW

At this stage, it will be more helpful for you to grasp the 'nature' of the 'Self of Tomorrow' rather than indulge in metaphysical speculation about what it is or is not.

After all, our true self is the person that the 'Self of Now' betrays when it indulges its greed, anger and illusion. Unfortunately, the 'Self of Tomorrow' is a stranger to most of us!

The clue, the great secret, is that the nature of the 'Self of Tomorrow' appears to be the same throughout time, irrespective of culture or location. No religion, time or people has a monopoly on the 'Self of Tomorrow'.

You probably would have seen this for yourself except for the fact that the modern world has convinced you that you can't trust your own senses and your own common sense.

It would seem that the establishment doesn't want you to know just how powerful you are.

We have been brainwashed!

LIFE PURPOSE AND LONG TERM FULFILMENT

The tragedy of life is realising how much of it you've wasted. As Saint Sheryl Crow said in her song, 'Soak up the Sun', ***"It's not having what you want, it's wanting what you've got!"***

When you look at the world through the 'Self of Tomorrow' every moment of your life is precious. Every breath that you take is a miracle.

When I look back at my life, through the terrible times, I can see that the only reason those times were so hard was because I wasted all the opportunities that life presented to me.

My life seemed terrible because I wasn't looking at reality, only at my own psychosis.

Right now I'm writing this book on the second structural edit. I'm stressed and I've got a headache. When the price of oil crashed so did my offshore career. I have to somehow make a living to support my family.

In the pit of my stomach, self-doubt, shame and a sense of failure threaten to consume me.

This is one reality. This is the Black Wolf.

Beneath these feelings and my idea of myself, there is a quiet clear lake of love. As I ignore the Black Wolf, I can hear the peace of the mountains outside.

My darling wife is working behind me. The sun is shining through the window. My puppy is snoring on her bed in my office. My 'Self of Tomorrow' is confident in the skills I have and the importance of this message. This is the White Wolf.

I know that the wisdom that has saved me can save other people. The modern world has never needed this ancient message more.

Instead of focussing on my own fear, I remember the fun that my wife and I have had creating all the books that we've written. Through these projects, and our community, my wife knows just how invaluable she is. Instead of living the empty lonely life of a wife of an offshore engineer, she has spent the last two years knowing that I couldn't have written any of the books without her.

Looking at the world through the 'Self of Tomorrow' I know that I am fulfilling my life's purpose by helping you, dear reader. Together all of us are creating a world of lasting fulfilment. This is the nature of sharing. When we focus on receiving from life in order to share with others everything comes into focus.

Life is something like a kaleidoscope. Look at it one way and it's hell, look at it another and it's heaven. The choice is yours.

WHAT IS A RIGHTEOUS MAN?

I grew up in a family that was nominally 'Christian'. Have you ever noticed that it's the people who make a big deal of calling themselves 'Christian' who are usually the most unpleasant people you could ever meet. When I grew up, I made it a rule to try to avoid 'Christians' whenever I could.

It wasn't until I was studying at the Underwater Centre in Scotland in my early 20s, that I met a man who would challenge my anti-Christian prejudice. My instructor, John Penny, was famous in the diving industry for being a wild kind of guy. Some time previously, he had an accident whilst diving and should have been dead.

More surprised than anyone at his survival, he dedicated himself to the Christian God. I only learnt about his spirituality much later. He never really mentioned it at the time.

As a deeply troubled lad, more used to being kicked than praised, I found being around John Penny remarkable.

He brought the diving team together and made people feel calm when they were more inclined to panic.

I remember that he managed to talk one of the students from Nigeria through a flooded full-face mask exercise. He inspired such confidence that the lad got through the task on the seventh attempt. When we asked him why he looked so sick, he said that he'd drunk the salt water because he couldn't work out how to blow the mask clear with air.

All of my life I had been used to deeply negative people full of secret poison. They invariably found their power by belittling and judging other people. In all the time that I knew John Penny I can't remember one time that he judged anyone.

I came from a poor background and had taken years to save the money to be on that course. The Underwater Centre, which was possibly the world's most famous dive school, is based in Fort William in the Scottish Highlands.

One night out in town I met an Australian girl who was trying to find her Scottish roots. When I told John of my new romance he gave me the keys to his car without even thinking about it. My own father wouldn't have even sold me one if I'd needed to drive my mother to hospital.

After meeting John Penny I have tried to live up to his example of kindness and generosity. He never once lectured me, he never once tried to preach to me but he organically changed my life. There have been, and are, people like that all over the world.

'GOD' MUST HAVE A SENSE OF HUMOUR!

It doesn't seem to make a difference what kind of religious nonsense you choose to believe, the nature of a human being at Hollywood's position 'B' is always the same. (Differing only in degree.)

Maybe you believe that the King of Ethiopia is actually the God of the Hebrew Old Testament, as did Bob Marley.

Maybe you believe that a Hebrew Rabbi in the first century was a God who sacrificed himself to himself to pay for your sins, as did my friend John Penny.

It's possible that you believe that God demands animal and human sacrifice, as did the Jewish people. Many people today believe that it is the will of God that they kill each other in the name of a sixth century Arab warlord.

None of this nonsense seems to matter. If you can restrict and dissolve the 'Self of Now' the effect is exactly the same irrespective of your culture or your belief.

Maybe God has a fantastic sense of humour?

The important thing to note is that in all cultures and times, the world has produced people who are psychologically and spiritually at Hollywood's position 'B' despite their intellectual beliefs and not because of them.

We can assume therefore that Position B or 'Holistic Enlightenment' is a common human experience.

THE LEGEND OF THE RIGHTEOUS

All over the world, throughout history, nearly every culture enshrines the concept of the 'Righteous' person. Catholics call them Saints, in Hebrew they are called Tzadik, in Buddhism they are called Enlightened.

All of them share similar personalities and characteristics that actually agree with Hollywood's protagonist at position 'B'.

MR MIYAGI IN THE KARATE KID, IS THE SAME AS YODA IN STAR WARS

When we change the direction of our intention away from the 'Self of Now', outward toward the 'Matrix', it naturally dissolves the 'Self of Now' and what happens to our character seems to be universal phenomena and is independent of cultural programming.

We tend to connect to people on a more genuine level, we see them as though they are actually a part of our own family. (It is for this reason that priests are often called 'father'.)

We also seem to find a cheerful optimism that sees everything that happens as happening for the best.

There is a wonderful story of a Rabbi on a flight from America to Israel. Halfway through the flight the oxygen masks drop down as the plane begins to drop out of the sky. Everyone is screaming except the Rabbi. The man next to him is holding on the seat in front with white knuckles. He turns to the Rabbi, and shouts, "Rabbi! We're going to die! Why are you not screaming?"

The Rabbi smiles and turns to the young man, "Why should I scream? So far I'm in good health!"

The person who has crushed the 'Self of Now' is no longer separated from the world by his own idea of himself. He cannot help but see the other person's point of view.

People naturally feel happier around him or her.

The Tzadik, is always rooted in this very moment and sees it as an expression of the universe moving.

We transfer (project) this Holistic Enlightenment onto fictional characters in popular culture like in the film Karate Kid and Star Wars.

THE MYTH OF SPIRITUAL ENLIGHTENMENT

In India it is quite normal to see people defecate in the street. In fact, fifty percent of the people in India defecate in the open. Despite having a space program, in India you can wait for a train and watch people pooping on the tracks (1). In India pooping in the open is quite normal.

Another wonderful idea from India, that has proved far worse for the world as a whole, is the concept of 'Enlightenment'. This cross-cultural contamination has been made even worse by the spiritual constipation of our materialistic culture: we only have one word for an idea that would take a book to describe.

If the Buddha said that he was 'Moksha' he may have meant that he was released from the cycle of birth and death. Obviously his celebrations might have been a little premature. He may have said, 'Bodhi' or 'Prahna' depending on which school of Buddhism you study. In Zen, to achieve 'Kensho' is to see into the heart of one's true nature.

Each of these terms are predefined by the nature of their cultural and historical presuppositions and as such cannot really, by definition, describe the living experience.

Unfortunately, in the West we only have one word for 'Enlightenment' and it's gotten as contaminated as an Indian train track.

Enlightenment isn't something that you achieve, or realise. It's not like something that you become and then you're out. Rather it is something that you already are but the very moment that you think you have it you really don't!

If you feel an overwhelming urge to change your name, have your feet kissed and fix other people's problems, realise that it's just the universe telling you that you are going in the wrong direction.

Conversely, if you find yourself in a crowd looking adoringly up at a man sitting on chair carefully placed higher than you, realise that what you think you see in him is a reflection of what is already in you.

LEAVE FOR DÜSSELDORF

My flight had still not been called. All I could think about was the comparative luxury of Düsseldorf airport. In my feverish mind it had taken on the status of Shangri-La.

An air hostess came around with a bowl of sweets. As she handed them out, row-by-row, people were just grabbing handfuls. Not to be short-changed, the man next to me grabbed the bowl and refused to let it go. Inevitably a tug of war ensued.

The Air France hostess didn't have the experience of the girl in Baku. She didn't know when to give up and save herself.

She almost got pulled on top of us but resisted by putting her foot on the armrest between us. The small Turk sitting next to me could not withstand such Gallic determination. He gave up the sweet bowl and the air hostess at the same time.

She managed to save herself but not the sweets. She said something very rude in French and stormed back to the comparative safety of the boarding gate.

CHAPTER 7

****

EVERYTHING IS LIGHT

I was flying on a seaman's ticket, which on long haul flights is something of a death sentence. Amazingly, the hostess had taken pity on me and bumped me up to business class and a window seat. Take off for Düsseldorf had been smooth and as we raced toward a low Turkish sky, I watched rain clouds come to meet us.

I pulled the magazine out of the net in front of me and flicked through its slightly sticky pages. Almost by itself, it fell open to an obviously well read article about the Dalai Lama. His smile was exactly as it was the last time I saw him, so many years ago, in London. On that day, he'd just flown in from Nepal and had arrived in London on the morning of his appearance but despite that, when he entered the room, his happiness had been contagious, his presence felt like static electricity.

The plane jinked to the right as we passed silently through a layer of clouds and entered the canyons and castles of a thunderstorm. Rain dribbled down the window and I shivered. Touching the moisture on the window, I had an overwhelming urge to reach out and touch the lightening as it forked down toward the Earth.

In Tibetan Buddhism the thunderbolt is synonymous with Enlightenment. The Dorje, its artistic representation, is held in the right hand while the bell, which represents wisdom, is held in the left hand. The plane shook as a thunderclap ripped the sky apart. At that moment I realised that all living beings are just like clouds in an endless sky.

Materialists see human life as an accident of natural selection and our consciousness as an illusion.

Religions see life as a prison and themselves as the escape committee but they are all wrong.

Surely a life created and supported by the entire universe must have some meaning, some reason!

In that moment I knew that, *"We are individual but yet not separate, eternally connected but, at the same time, momentarily unique. The body is just the cloud that we can see but in reality we are a part of everything. Each moment of life is sacred because an entire universe has conspired to create it."*

As I write this in my notebook, I bite my pen and look out of the window at the now clear sky.

My words sound just like a thousand memes on Facebook. If you walk the streets of San Francisco and get hit by a car, I guarantee that it would be a Hybrid with something like those words on its bumper sticker. Since the 70s we have become numb to 'feelgood' spiritual BS because we hear so much of it!

We nod and share the post but we don't really believe it. Hell, we don't even try to understand it! Today we are surrounded by so much information that we have become immune to any idea we don't already hold. Why?

Because we have given up on hope and we've been trained to believe whatever we are told to believe. The 'government-controlled-media' makes an announcement, 'Science Says.....XYZ', and like Pavlov's dogs, we open our mind to be programmed.

It wasn't always like this! You do have a choice!

Let me give you a reason to want more than a life of slavery.

Let me give you a reason to hope! Let me burst the bubble of consensus science that keeps you a slave in your own life.

WHAT IS REAL?

If I told you that black was white would you believe me? No! I didn't think so.

If I told you that black was white and wrote a mathematical equation on the board, would you believe me then? No, but you might start to doubt yourself.

The sad truth is that in the twentieth century we've been programmed to not even trust our own common sense. The newspapers and the internet are full of stories that tell us what foods to eat or what foods not to eat.

They tell us what is good for our health and what is bad for our health. In my lifetime I have seen them contradict everything they said when I was a boy.

If you take the time to investigate the facts, nobody will listen to you! The power of the consensus will shut you down.

Unfortunately, the truth does matter! Ignoring the truck that hits you won't stop you getting dead!

If you want to reclaim the joy you had as a child you are going to have to take the 'red pill' and wake up to a different perception of reality than the one they gave you.

If you can stick with me to the end of this chapter, I'm going to prove to you that you are a cloud and at the same time the infinite sky.

EINSTEIN GIVES BIRTH TO A CULT!

Darwin wasn't the only man responsible for the toxic materialism that dominated the twentieth century. A small German clerk working in a Swiss Patent Office, almost by accident, persuaded an entire planet to abandon their own logic and common sense.

He was a dedicated socialist and loudly advocated for the establishment of a one-world government. The name of this odious scruffy little man was Albert Einstein and he was fascinated by light.

We have been programmed to believe that Einstein, like Darwin, was a genius; not many people have ever had the courage to ask why!

Einstein invented nothing and yet his theories directly, and indirectly, affect how you live your life.

THE CONNECTED UNIVERSE BEFORE EINSTEIN

Before Einstein, scientists working in the field of electromagnetics believed that the universe consisted of an electromagnetic sea that connected everything. They called that sea the 'Aether'.

Scientists like Sir Isaac Newton, Michael Faraday, James Clerk Maxwell, Nicola Tesla and Hendrik Lorentz assumed that light moved as a wave through the Aether. In 1887, Michelson-Morely set out to measure the speed of the Earth through the Aether.

They expected to measure a speed of about 30 km/sec but they actually measured a speed of less than 10 km/sec (1). It looked like the Earth was stationary and they thought that was a major problem. They decided to call it a null result and blame their equipment.

EINSTEIN PULLS THE PLUG

Einstein got around the problem of the 'stationary' Earth by getting rid of Aether altogether. His theories were based on an old idea that the universe was made up of separate particles rather than a unifying Aether.

It follows that if the world is made up of separate particles we have no connection to anything. Einstein taught us that we are all fundamentally and irrevocably alone!

Unfortunately, Einstein's theories were not supported by logic or observed reality. Prior to Einstein, physics dealt with the real world of objects and tried to explain reality. Einstein didn't even try!

Einstein, more than any other man, turned science into the religion of theoretical mathematics.

In the modern world, when someone commits suicide they tend to think that their lives are of little worth. Usually they assume that their death will affect nobody but themselves. They believe that they are disconnected from the world.

What if that wasn't true? What if your life was as important to me as my own? What if we are all diminished by the suffering of any single living being? What if Einstein was wrong?

DARKNESS OR LIGHT

When I said that I was writing a book called 'Quantum Mechanics For Your Soul', a lot of people said, "What has Quantum Physics got to do with spirituality?"

That question tells us a lot about our common assumptions, particularly our assumptions about science:

- *Science has nothing to do with us.*

- *Science has nothing to do with spirituality.*

- *Quantum is not something for ordinary people to be concerned with.*

Einstein published his papers in 1905 and started a war. On one side Einstein, and his priests, insisted that light is made up of separate particles. He insisted that space curves and time is relative. On the other side of this war was Nicola Tesla and he said,

"Only the existence of a field of force can account for the motions of the bodies as observed, and its assumption dispenses with space curvature. All literature on this subject is futile and destined to oblivion. So are all attempts to explain the workings of the universe without recognising the existence of the Aether and the indispensable function it plays in the phenomena."

Nikola Tesla July 10, 1937. Written for his 81st birthday speech.

Nicola Tesla invented Alternating Current electricity, fluorescent light bulbs, X-Rays, Radio, Wi-Fi, the Electric Motor and Laser. Nicola Tesla almost single-handedly created the world in which you live today (2). Einstein, on the other hand, invented nothing.

It would seem that we have two choices! Either Einstein was right and the universe is made up of separate particles or Tesla was right and we live in a sea of light called the Aether.

Your life, how you see yourself and how you deal with the people you love, is a direct product of your assumptions about the world around you.

In order to understand the implications of the answers it is first necessary that you understand the profundity of the questions.

When I later say that every atom in you is connected to every atom in the universe, you won't just read it as an empty and meaningless meme. In fact, you will see it as a fundamental principle of your life. When you see life exactly as it is, you can't just go on living as a slave to the system.

THE (QUANTUM) SUB-ATOMIC UNIVERSE

Have a look at your hand. Touch the back of one hand with the fingers of the other. It feels real doesn't it?

Democritus was a Greek philosopher who lived in four hundred BC and he was the first person to come up with the idea of the 'atom'. He thought that if you could break an object down into small enough parts eventually you would get to a point where you can't divide it anymore. (The word 'atom' means indivisible).

What is important to realise is that only 1% of an atom is 'material' the other 99% is space.

"Everything we call real is made of things that cannot be regarded as real."
N. Bohr.

When you touch your hand only 1% of it could be considered as 'physical'. The only reason that it 'feels' real to you is because the atoms in your hand are resonating in a way that you experience it as solid.

Change the energy of water molecules and they become water vapour or ice. If you change your own energy, say by falling into water from a great height, when you hit the water it's like hitting concrete.

The world you experience every day is an infinite electromagnetic sky, whose 'physicality' is entirely dependent on rhythm and spin.

SHOW ME AN ATOM!
Everything starts with the atom (3).

If the atom is just a separate and discrete particle then we truly are alone in a meaningless universe.

The truth is that after 80 years of investigation, consensus science cannot present a photo or a drawing of the **structure** of one hydrogen atom. Hydrogen atoms consist of only one proton and one electron so, in theory, it shouldn't be too hard!

If you take a class in electronics you might be given any number of various and conflicting descriptions of the structure of the atom. Let me explain why!

In 1911, **Ernst Rutherford** came up with the planetary model of the atom by shooting alpha particles at a sheet of gold. He posited the idea that the electron orbits the proton like the Moon orbits around the Earth (4). Nobody could explain why the negative electron doesn't crash into the positive proton, as it should.

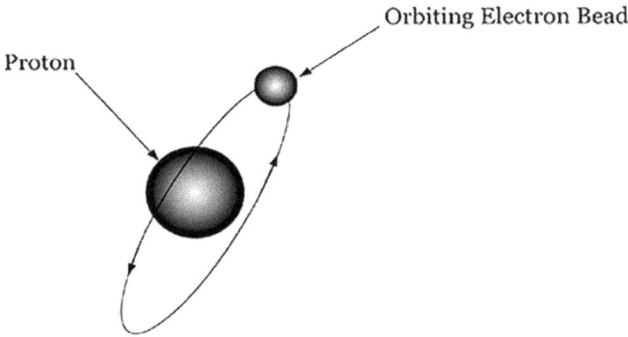

[Image 3: Rutherford's orbiting bead model of the atom.]

Niels Bohr suggested that the electron spontaneously jumps to a new energy band around the proton but failed to explain why that might be so. This is where we get the term 'Quantum Jump' (5).

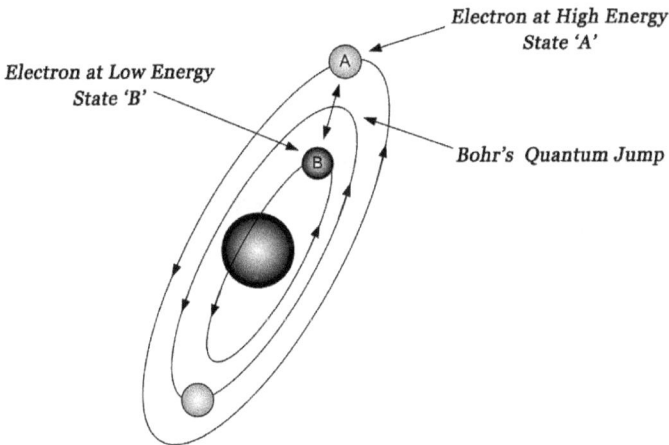

[Image 4: Niels Bohr's model of the atom.]

Louis De Broglie suggested that the electron is stretched around its orbit in waves. Why an electron should follow a wave or why it should be restrained to an orbit was a mystery not addressed. This vision of the atom has been adapted over the last three quarters of a century so that we now have balloons by which a negative electron is understood to pass through a positive proton. Despite the fact that we know that this is physically impossible.

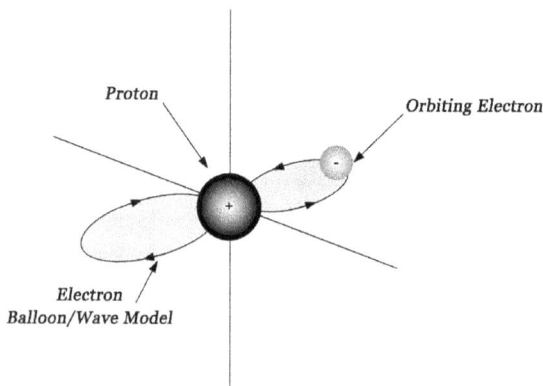

[Image 5: Louis De Broglie's model of the atom]

Erwin Schrodinger and **Max Born** posited the idea of a 'cloud' of probability around the proton. Obviously this is just a different way of describing Rutherford's orbiting bead model.

This version of the atom seems to be in fashion at the moment. The problem is that consensus science is trying to sell us a movie while telling us it's a snapshot.

At any point in time, it should be possible to say exactly where the 'electron' is, but all attempts to photograph the atom seems to describe either a balloon or a dandelion type structure.

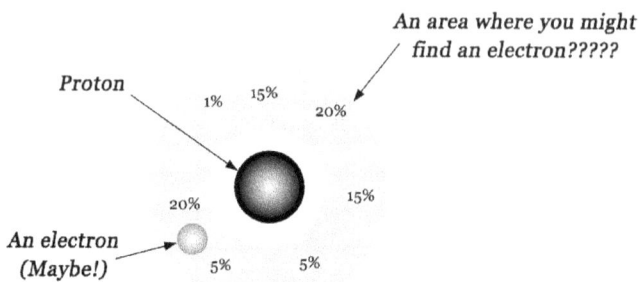

[Image 6: Shrodinger and Born probability model of the atom.]

SELECTIVE CONFUSION

So which is it? Is an atom a planet with orbiting beads or a balloon with a skin?

The priests of consensus science make their pronouncements and we assume that they have all the answers. You would think that after all these years that these smug elitists would be able to tell us what an atom looks like! Not only don't they know what an atom looks like but they lack the strength of character to even admit that they don't know.

Ionisation and electric current are usually explained in terms of the 'bead' model of the atom. While the 'balloon' model of the atom is used to explain how two atoms could physically bond together to form a molecule (6).

We know that molecular chemists work with an atomic object that plainly has a 'skin' and the picture of two colliding gold atoms presented by the Brookhaven National Laboratory clearly shows a 'dandelion-like' object with a kind of 'skin'.

If we leave it to the priests of the cult of Einstein, the sub-atomic world would forever remain beyond our understanding. Thankfully there is another kid on the block.

A CIA SPY SAVES THE WORLD

Sr Guillermo Gaede is an Argentinian Physicist, Engineer and CIA Spy. He came up with an answer to Einstein's insanity. His Electromagnetic Rope theory builds on Maxwell's equations and the incredible work of Nicola Tesla (7). While Einstein and his priests have left us in confusion with either a particle or a wave, Gaede offers us a logical third choice: an Electromagnetic Rope.

The Electromagnetic Rope hypothesis posits that electromagnetic threads fork at the boundary of an atom and the magnetic 'thread' forms the shell of the atom. The EM Ropes from every other atom in the universe converge on the atom and form an 'urchin' like star that we call a 'proton'. The surface of this shell resembles a ball of yarn or a dandelion, which might also be called a balloon.

With the EM Rope hypothesis the observable properties of the atom finally have a coherent explanation that we can all understand. We will also find that this hypothesis solves so many other problems that consensus science studiously ignores.

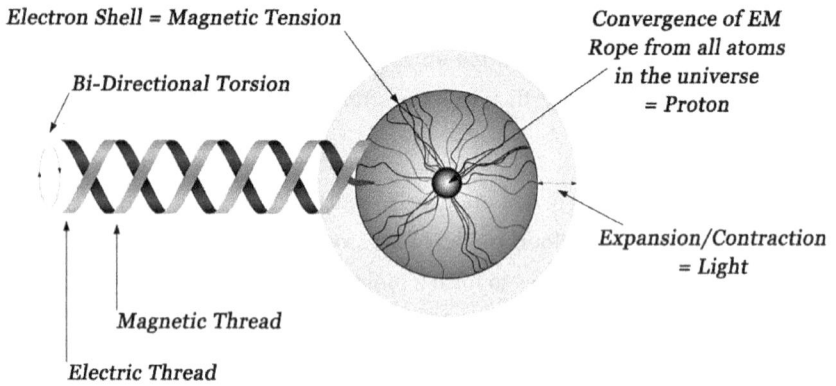

Electron Shell = Magnetic Tension

Bi-Directional Torsion

Convergence of EM
Rope from all atoms
in the universe
= Proton

Expansion/Contraction
= Light

Magnetic Thread

Electric Thread

[Image 7: EM Rope model of the atom.]

The EM Rope hypothesis provides a neat explanation as to why an electron is bound to the proton. It also elegantly explains the phenomenon of 'Quantum Jump', where an electron jumps between orbits. As we will see later, the EM Rope hypothesis also explains the very nature of the proton and its relationship to light.

Now if you look at your hand, you can easily imagine that the atoms in your hand are connected to the atoms in the air around it. The only thing that divides them is the power of magnetic attraction. Welcome to the sub-atomic universe.

A CONNECTED UNIVERSE

If you have external speakers plugged into a MacBook Pro, as you put your hand near the body of your computer you will hear a background hissing. This white noise is the product of the field of energy that surrounds your body.

Astronomers have noted that the universe itself gives off background radiation. In every square centimetre around you, 1% is generating white noise that you can hear and see on your TV.

In 1965, Arno A. Penzias and Robert W. Wilson of Bell Laboratories discovered that the universe has background microwave radiation.

It was immediately assumed to be evidence for the Big Bang Theory (8) but was it?

It never seemed to occur to anyone that it might be evidence of the Aether that Tesla had tried to tell them about, fifty years before. Instead consensus science came up with a fairy story about something coming from nothing.

All of the major discoveries in electromagnetics were made by men that believed in the *Aether* but were never really able to suggest a physical model that would explain its existence, until now!

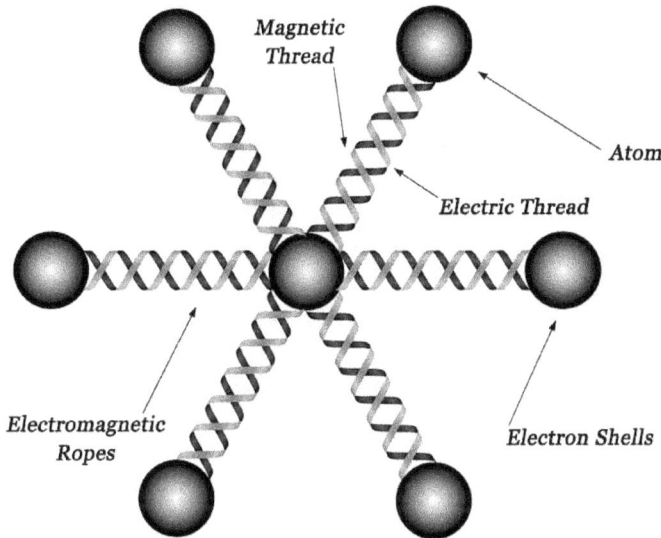

[Image 8: EM Rope model of electromagnetic aether.]

The EM Rope Hypothesis suggests that every atom in the universe is connected to every other atom and that white noise on your TV is evidence of it.

Above is a diagram that explains the connected universe.

When Einstein was asked to explain how a physical object could be compelled to move through space without any visible means of coercion, he shrugged his shoulders and called it, 'Spooky action at a distance'.

Einstein was committed to the idea that the universe was made up of separate particles so he had no logical way to explain how a magnet pulls an object through space.

Magnetic force is another way that you and I can confirm that we are indeed connected to everything in the universe.

SPOOKY ACTION AT A DISTANCE

There are four forms of physical attraction that we observe in the real world:

1. Local Magnetic Attraction.

2. Attraction caused by static electricity on organic material.

3. Planetary Orbit.

4. Gravity.

Any explanation of observed phenomena should include some kind of physical model that adequately explains all four manifestations of physical attraction. Unfortunately, if you wait for consensus science to give you an answer, you're going to be waiting for a long time.

If you've ever asked about magnetic attraction at school you would have been given some diagrams of magnetic regions and lines of force but this is a description of some aspects of the phenomena, not an explanation.

1. LOCAL MAGNETIC ATTRACTION

Einstein didn't really address the phenomenon of local magnetic attraction.

Some lecturers try to explain this phenomenon as a form of 'Quantum Entanglement' but that is not really what is meant by the term.

Others have tried to apply Einstein's hypothesis of warped space to a local magnet (more of which later) but the fact that magnetic objects are affected while non-magnetic objects are not disproves this explanation.

The standard high school explanation is that a magnet has a 'magnetic field' that has 'lines of force', which attract one object to another. Obviously, once again this is just a description and not an explanation. If you are still awake, you might ask what 'field' means or what causes 'lines of force'.

If you do you may well be given a fail grade and kicked out of the class.

It was through my attempts to understand magnetic attraction, when I was studying to become a Technical Authority in electromagnetics, that I stumbled across EM Rope hypothesis. It is the only theory that can explain the phenomena of magnetic 'fields', 'lines of force' and attraction with the same elegant model.

To understand magnetic attraction we need to apply the EM Rope hypothesis and see that a magnetic field is nothing more than EM Ropes emanating from an object (9).

Imagine, if you will, two children playing skipping rope. If one child follows the other they will both be rotating counter-clockwise from our perspective. As the following child comes too close to his friend his rope will interfere with the rope in front. The effect of this interference is that the two children will be pulled together. If you reverse the rope spin of one child, when the ropes hit they will push the other rope away.

This over-simplification still comfortably explains magnetic attraction in principal and can account for all four examples of 'action at a distance'.

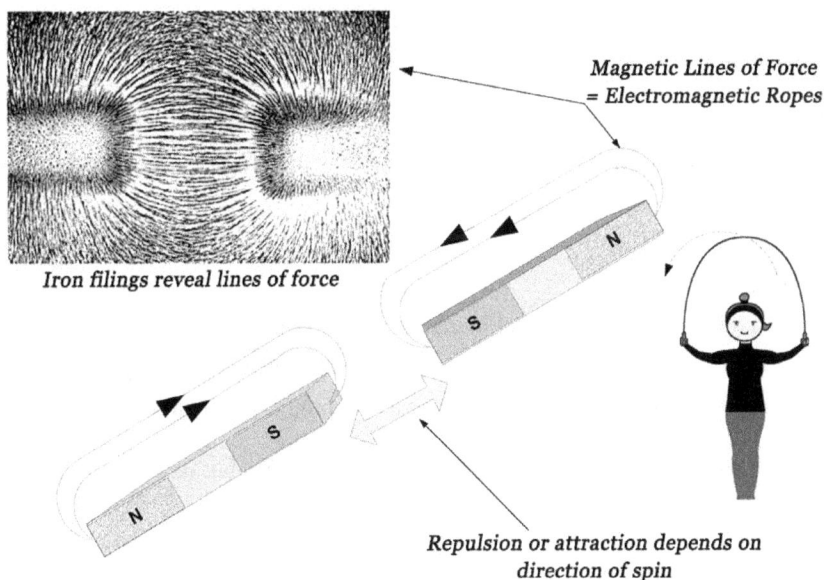

Iron filings reveal lines of force

Magnetic Lines of Force = Electromagnetic Ropes

Repulsion or attraction depends on direction of spin

[Image 9: EM Rope model of local magnetic attraction.]

WHY THIS MATTERS!

Quantum's inability to answer the most basic of children's questions gives us the power to take back responsibility for our own reality. We can finally see that the emperor has no clothes.

How we perceive the world around us is a direct product of magnetic attraction. The fact that your hand feels this book to be solid is a product of the magnetic attraction of each of the molecules that form your hand and this book. The sea of light within which you live your life only 'appears' to be made up of separate units of mass. In reality, at the atomic level we are all intimately linked together.

2. ATTRACTION CAUSED BY STATIC ELECTRICITY ON ORGANIC MATERIAL

Theoretically, only electrically conductive materials should be susceptible to static electricity but we find that paper and rubber (both poor electrical conductors) are easily attracted.

We also find that organic objects like water, which should not be influenced by magnetic attraction, are in fact displaced due to static electricity.

The standard explanation of 'polarisation' is really only a description of electric induction and does not account for physical movement.

When we apply EM Rope theory we can see that any excitement of electromagnetic ropes is likely to produce attraction at a distance as the EM Rope Matrix seeks to re-establish balance.

WHY THIS MATTERS!

We can all observe the fact that living beings generate an electrical 'force' around them that often reacts to nearby objects. My wife, for instance, often gets an electric shock if she touches me when I'm pushing a shopping trolley in a supermarket.

Most of us have experiences of static electricity everyday but we've been trained to never wonder about it.

In the next chapter we will look at the work of Dr Konstantin Korotkov on the Human Energy Field (HEF) more commonly called the aura.

3. PLANETARY ORBIT

Einstein rarely pontificated about practical matters where his theories could easily be disproved. He tended to limit his work to theorising about space and planets.

He suggested that planetary orbit was caused by the density of a planet warping the fabric of space-time and turning it into a cosmic roulette wheel. According to Einstein the Moon is constrained in its orbit by the curvature of space (10).

There are a few problems with this idea:

1. Einstein's theory depends on space being made up of separate and discrete particles. He offered no explanation as to how separate sand-like particles suddenly turned into a membrane-like fabric.

2. Neither did he offer a mechanism of how space-time might actually act upon a physical object. How can 'nothing' act upon something without friction?

3. Einstein's model assumes a universal gravity that would turn forward momentum into an orbit. Several planets orbit in different planes so prove this theory false.

4. As $E=mc^2$ denies the existence of an Aether, in what medium does space/time exist in? How can nothing be distorted by something?

5. Einstein's model of curved space cannot account for the observed behaviour of planets and galaxies, so theoretical physicists invented the idea of Dark Matter and Black Holes to account for the failures of Einstein's calculations.

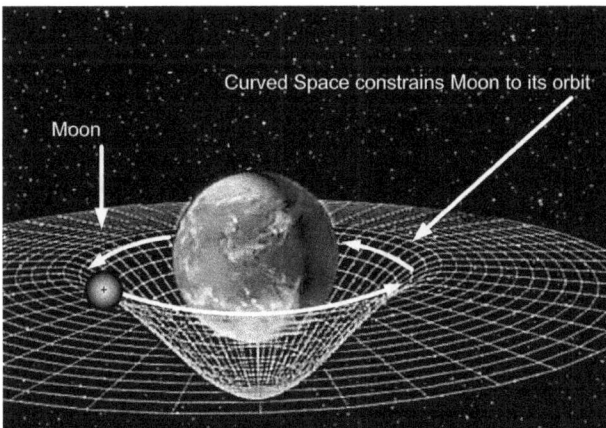

[Image 10: Einstein's curved space explanation for planetary orbit.]

EM ROPE ON PLANETARY MOVEMENT

In contrast to Einstein's illogical theory of general relativity, the EM Rope hypothesis offers us an elegant and simple explanation of how a moon is constrained in an elliptical orbit dictated by the relative mass of each object and the amount of ropes that are able to directly pull on the object. The further away an object is the less EM Ropes have an effective angle from which to pull.

EM Rope hypothesis can account for the movement of planets and galaxies without the necessity of inventing supportive theories to account for its deficiencies. This fact in itself proves the validity of the hypothesis and the connected nature of the universe.

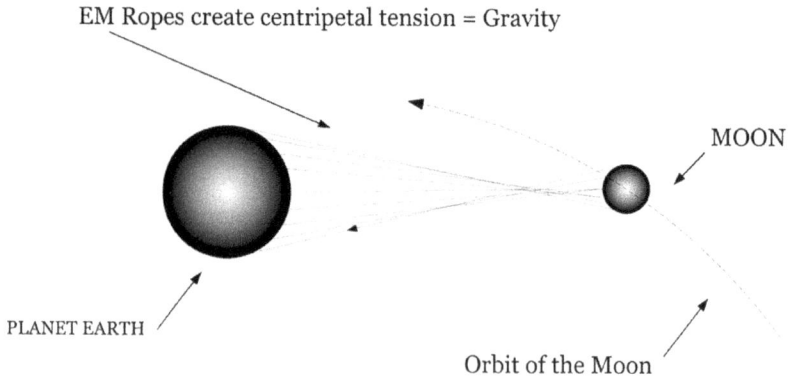

EM Ropes create centripetal tension = Gravity

MOON

PLANET EARTH

Orbit of the Moon

[Image 11: EM Rope model of planetary orbit.]

WHY THIS MATTERS?

Of all of Einstein's ideas, curved space, as an answer to planetary movement, was the one that seemed to convince ordinary people to stop asking awkward questions.

The absurdity of general and special relativity confirmed 'consensus scientists' as the new priesthood of the big state. A wedge was driven between ordinary people and the world around them. More important than that, ordinary people were intimidated into believing whatever the establishment told them to believe.

4. GRAVITY

As we have seen, in order to try to explain gravity and therefore planetary movement, Einstein's primary model was a curvature in space-time. However, in his 1916 paper, he discusses another model called 'Gravitational Waves' in order to explain action at a distance.

So Einstein needed two models in order to explain the observable phenomena of planetary movement and gravity. This anomaly would normally be enough to prove a theory is false but nobody had the guts to tell him.

Let's have a look and see if we think his ideas held any water.

Einstein stated that his gravitational waves would travel at the speed of light.

As your weight is a product of gravity, we can easily debunk Einstein's ridiculous theory.

For the sake of argument, let's say that you are standing on the surface of the Earth at location 'A' and your weight is X.

Now imagine that you are standing on a platform two miles above the surface of the Earth at location 'B' and your weight would now be X-y.

We have all seen scientists in the space station flying around and this is due to their relative distance from the Earth's gravity. So it is obvious that you would weigh less at location 'B'.

Let's assume that you are teleported between locations 'A' and 'B' instantaneously. Your weight at those locations would also change instantaneously. You would not have to wait for the gravitational waves lagging behind you at the speed of light to catch up with you.

Recently it was announced by consensus scientists (who were in danger of losing their funding) that 'gravitational waves' had been detected and lauded as proof of Einstein's theory.

Consensus science states as fact that two black holes merged a 'long-time ago and far away' and created 'gravitational waves'. It is important to note that NASA describes a 'black hole' as a physical object, while the Max Planck Institute of physics describes them as **not** being a 'tangible object' but a 'region'.

Because they are lost within their maths they can't see what is obvious to any independent observer: that they don't know what they've found or where it's from!

Professor Oleg D. Jefimenko questions Einstein's theories in his book, *'Electromagnetic Retardation and Theory of Relativity'* and refuted the 'Gravitational Wave' hypothesis.

Embarrassingly, Ken L. Wheeler has produced a huge archive of material on electromagnetics as Theoria Apophasis and neatly demonstrates that the Enhanced LIGO found only a local electromagnetic wave and, as proof, he recreated the effect using two magnets (11).

WHY MAGNETS MATTER?

The foundation of the cultural power that the 'establishment' holds over us is held in the hands of consensus science.

The problem is not with the observations that have been made over the last hundred years, but rather, the worldview that is inculcated by the explanations with which we've been indoctrinated.

The sub-atomic universe and the way that one object is attracted or repelled by another is a way that everyone can intuitively grasp a more holistic worldview. Within the EM Rope hypothesis we can glimpse a world where each of us is connected to everything.

Perhaps more important than that, by debunking the monopoly that consensus science claims for itself, we can help people to feel empowered to once again think for themselves.

DOES LIGHT BEND AND WHY YOU SHOULD CARE?

We have examined the nature of the sub-atomic universe and we've looked at the questions consensus science can't answer. I believe that we've suggested some compelling alternatives to the explanations usually offered.

You may have some concept now of the two standard physical models offered by quantum science to account for the observed phenomena: discrete particles versus waves. As we have already mentioned, the EM Rope hypothesis offers us a third alternative.

From the comfort of your own living room you can prove for yourself that light doesn't travel as a wave, nor as a particle and definitively not as a packet. You will see that light actually travels as an electromagnetic rope.

In 1704, the Reverend John Michell, an English clergyman and natural philosopher, reasoned that light would be subject to planetary gravity but never tested his theory.

Sir Isaac Newton believed that light consisted of physical particles so logically assumed that gravity would have an effect on it but wrote little on the subject.

Throughout the seventeenth and eighteenth century, light was one of the most popular subjects of investigation.

Consensus science still cannot logically and coherently explain the nature of light, as they cannot describe the atom.

To understand the true nature of light is to understand the universe. The only elegant explanation of all the observed phenomena we have detailed so far is the EM Rope hypothesis. Certainly, as evidence of the validity of the EM Rope hypothesis, the nature of light is the most assessable and easy for the layman to grasp.

So in order to understand the profundity of the answer let's follow the history of the question.

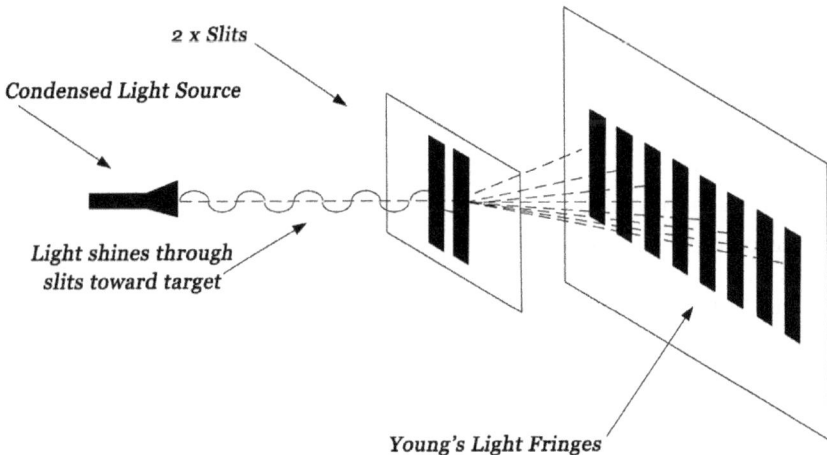

[Image 12: Thomas Young's famous slit experiment of 1801.]

Thomas Young was an English doctor. In 1801, he created the double slit experiment in order to try to understand the nature of light. Young expected to shine a light through two slits and see two patches of light on the screen, instead he saw many. He called these 'ghost' images, 'fringes'.

Young concluded that light was a wave and moved as if it were a liquid. He created several sketches of 'Wave Interference' based on his observations of waves in fluid in order to explain the fringes of light, which he had observed. The only way that he could think to explain the fringes was to say that light travelled as a wave.

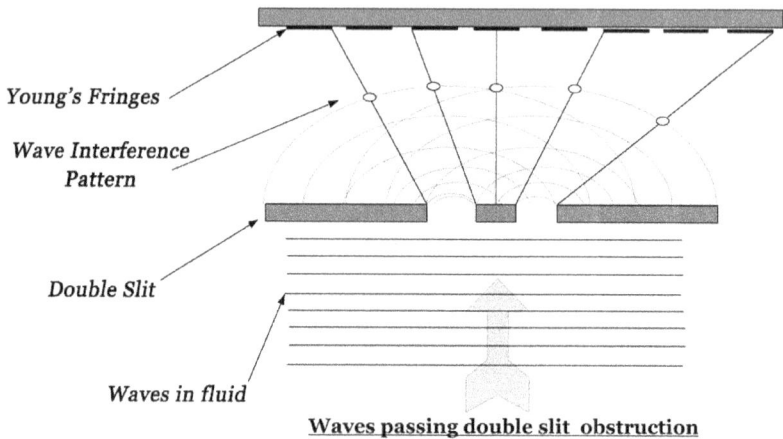

Waves passing double slit obstruction

[Image 13: Young's assumption of lightwave interference patterns.]

Einstein, on the other hand, was committed to the idea that light consists of discrete particles and would not accept Young's explanation. Einstein's explanation for Young's light fringes suggested that light, travelling as particles, would ricochet from the corners of the two slits and be deflected in order to create 'fringes'.

The fact that everybody accepted Einstein's ridiculous explanation and didn't try to disprove it says a lot about the power of the consensus.

As physics has moved further and further away from objective reality, it has forced the world to fit into the narrow confines of its theory rather than changing the theory to fit the reality of physical observations.

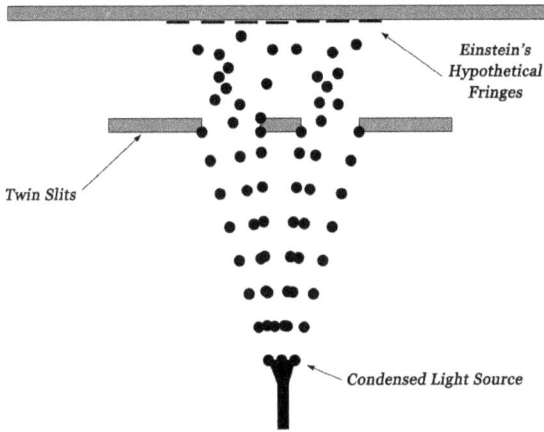

[Image 14: Einstein's light-as-a-particle explanation for 'fringes'.]

Until Einstein, science was something that 'ladies and gentlemen' of leisure and curiosity indulged in. They were not beholden to the state or to universities for funds, so they were able to follow the evidence toward conclusions.

Einstein unwittingly handed science over to a faceless army of sycophants who now live in the pocket of the State and big business. They inhabit an echo chamber full of one opinion and ignore evidence unless it supports their foregone conclusions.

DOES LIGHT BEND?

A huge step toward our dystopian future was taken when Einstein predicted that light would be deflected around the mass of a planet by the curvature of space-time.

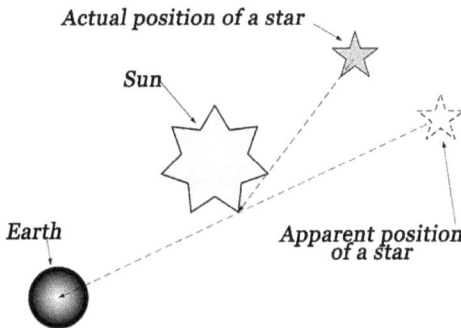

[Image 15: Light bent by the assumed curvature of space.]

His theory of general relativity finally cut the mooring line that had been anchoring physics to the real world.

Theoretical mathematics now uses physical terms interchangeably so that no one can be sure what anyone is really talking about. Dimensions become coordinates and a point becomes a location. Even better, a line is now defined by two lines or it can be the distance between two objects.

Within all this confusion, nobody can explain why light seems to bend around corners.

It is easy for anyone to confirm that light bends around objects and seems to shine around corners. Just watch the rising sun over the mountains and you will see that light seems to expand around corners and does not restrict itself to a direct line from its source.

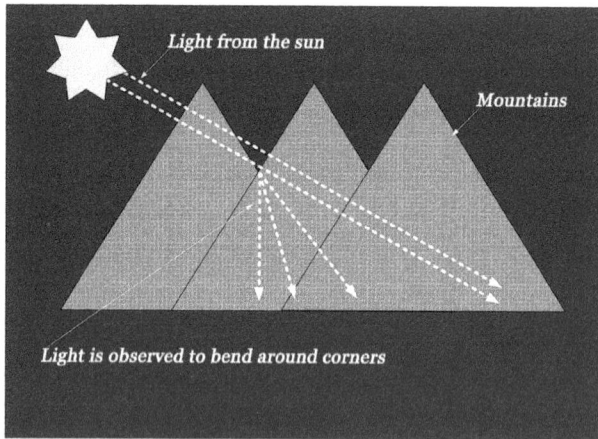

[Image 16: Observed reality — light bends around corners.]

Neither Young's wave model nor Einstein's particle theory can explain the observed behaviour of light.

GAEDE'S NEEDLE OF LIGHT

Gaede created a simple experiment to disprove both the wave and the particle theory of light. He noticed that a fluid passing a single post does not create an interference pattern. He determined to recreate Young's slit experiment but instead of using two slits he decided to use only a single needle and a laser light, in order to test Young's wave hypothesis.

You can easily repeat Gaede's simple light experiment for yourself.

Get a good quality laser light pointer and a needle stuck in a cotton reel. Position the light a few metres from a plain wall. Between the light and the wall, position the needle so its body bisects the laser light. You will see on the wall Young's fringes of light.

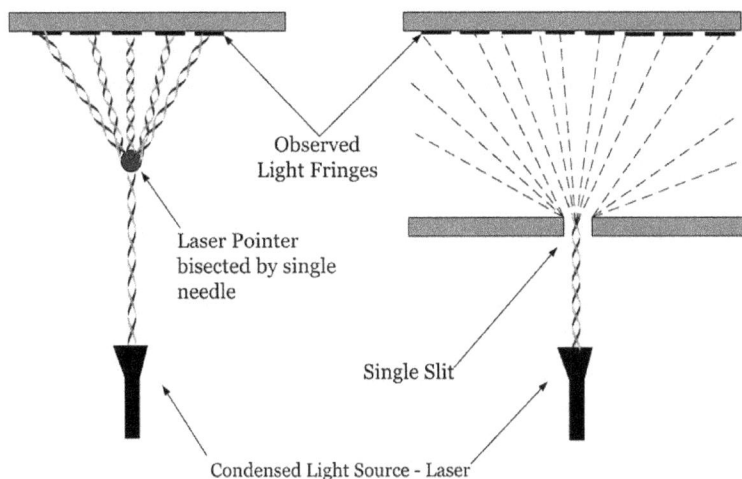

Observed Light Fringes

Laser Pointer bisected by single needle

Single Slit

Condensed Light Source - Laser

[Image 17: Gaede's needle experiment single object creating fringes.]

Obviously fluid dynamics does not suggest that interference fringes are caused by a single object so we **can't** conclude that light moves as a wave. Neither can we conclude that Einstein's bouncing particles account for the fringes of light you see on the wall.

The truth is that the only coherent and logical model that can account for all of the phenomena that we've discussed is the EM Rope Hypothesis.

Just to summarise: Gaede creates interference fringes around a single needle. This disproves the theory that light is a wave. Standard waves would not create interference around a single point. Neither would particles create the observed fringes.

This experiment neatly proves that light travels as an electromagnetic rope between atoms that are always connected. This explains why light appears to go around corners. This explains rationally why light passing around a planet appears to be curved. We now have no need of Einstein's 'curved space'.

WHY DOES THIS MATTER?

In the brave new world of Steven Hawking (Einstein's inheritor), universes are infinite but light speed cannot be exceeded. We are forever trapped alone in an entirely pointless and accidental world.

The orthodoxy of scientific consensus has limited and effectively blocked any research that it views as heretical.

When Professor Halton Arp found evidence that the assumptions about 'Red Shift' (light changes colour as it recedes away) were wrong, based on his work on Quasars (super bright light source), his career was destroyed by the establishment.

It is vital that we understand that 'scientists' have become the new 'priesthood' and just like the Church that went before, they are just men.

None of this would matter if the world created by our governments and the new priesthood of science was the utopia that they promised, but it is not.

LIGHT IS THE ONLY REALITY

The sub-atomic universe is a universe of light. The Holistic Universe unites magnetic attraction, the behaviour of light and atomic structure into one elegant theory.

These examples help us to visualise a universe where physical matter is really only light vibrating at a certain frequency and is inherently devoid of form.

This explains how all living beings are like a rain cloud within an electromagnetic sea.

From a distance we appear to be solid and separate but on investigation we continue to be a part of the 'sky' and therefore connected to all the other clouds.

In our case the 'sky' we are a part of is infinite and the cloud is our physical form.

When the Dalai Lama tells us that we are all connected, we just nod and smile indulgently; we wish it were true but can't see how it possibly could be.

I have detailed the scientific reasons why these spiritual statements are true and I have tried to keep my explanations as brief as possible. I am not suggesting that I have a monopoly on truth or that my opinion should be taken as gospel.

All I am saying is that there is enough scientific evidence to suggest that not one more person should die alone while feeling that their lives are of no value.

Our feelings of separation and loneliness can now be seen to be just a fantasy created by the illusion of the 'Self of Now'.

ARRIVE DUSSELDORF

As the wheels hit the runway, the engines screamed in reverse and my magazine slid under the seat in front of me. I had been thinking about the Dalai Lama and wondering how he manages to never give in to hate. It was strange because I'd not thought of him in years.

The seatbelt light went out and everyone rushed to fill the aisle. Like a pack of dogs on the hunt you could sense the tension in our little tubular world. Stuck in the window seat, hidden from view I took the opportunity to indulge my favourite sport and watch people live their lives.

A small Imam was trying to wrestle a bag stuffed with presents from the overhead locker. A tall man reached across and helped him land the bag that was almost as big as the Imam. Everyone smiled and I could feel the tension fall away.

As the plane began to empty, the line of people blocking the aisle in front of me made their way to the front of the plane. Just as I passed the last loo before the exit, my eye was caught by a young Korean man with a military haircut waiting at the entrance to first class. He was eyeing me suspiciously. Behind him I noticed the flash of familiar maroon beneath the smiling eyes. He was wearing the kind of eyeshade favoured by card sharks and middle-aged golfers but his eyeshade was maroon like his robes.

I stopped in my tracks to make way for the 14th Dalai Lama. As he headed for the cabin door he paused and looked back at me. I wondered if he recognised me but quickly discounted the idea, 'How could he possibly remember a face in a room from so long ago'? He smiled and nodded as though he knew exactly what I was thinking. His bodyguard was obviously impatient. The Dalai Lama put his hand on the young man's arm to reassure him. I blinked and he was gone.

In that moment, I knew that my new understanding was something that the Dalai Lama had been living with for a long time.

CHAPTER 8

THE MATRIX

So I'd finally arrived in Düsseldorf airport, and expected to have two hours to kill before my connection to London. I knew a wonderful soba noodle stand, in a quiet corner of the airport, run by a lovely man from Vietnam. I hoped to have a late breakfast with him, as we both loved to talk about Vung Tau, the seaside village of his birth. That would leave me time, before my next flight, to buy my wife a present.

I'd just finished a wonderful bowel of Pho and was wishing that you could still smoke in airports when I had a feeling of panic, like one of those dreams where you are trying to call someone you love but can never remember the number or get the phone to work. I'd been so jet-lagged that I'd forgotten to call my wife and let her know that I had arrived safely in Europe. I reached for my phone.

Almost at the same split second my telephone vibrated in my hand and began to ring.

"Thank God you answered! I was so worried," she said tearfully. My heart sunk to my boots because I couldn't believe that I'd been so selfish.

"I was just going to call you darling! I had the phone in my hand!" I added somewhat lamely.

"We're so connected!" She said, as she always does. "We always seem to call each other at the same time."

Most people who work away from home on a regular basis find that they are subconsciously connected to their loved ones.

Most people experience a non-verbal, non-physical connectedness to their loved ones but we've been taught to ignore it.

Telepathy, then, is a normal part of life but one that 'consensus science' studiously ignores.

It's a sign of how deep the rot has gone that there are, today, so few scientists who have anything like a natural curiosity about the world beyond the consensus. They, and we, have been brainwashed to ignore our own observations about the world around us.

Professor Rupert Sheldrake makes observations, forms hypothesis and then rigorously tests the hypothesis. He got his PhD in biochemistry at Cambridge and became a fellow of Clare College.

Once upon a time, in a kinder world, we called men like Sheldrake, 'scientists'. Today lesser men call him a heretic because the implications of his work are so dangerous to the power of the establishment.

Even his TEDx talk at Whitechapel was banned, despite being incredibly popular.

As Deepak Chopra said, "Professor Rupert Sheldrake's contributions (to science) will be recognised one day on the same level as those of Newton."

THE NATURE OF THE MATRIX - MORPHIC RESONANCE

We have seen that we live in a Holistic Universe made up entirely of electromagnetic threads, which appear to form a universal aether exactly as Nicola Tesla described. Let's call that the 'structure' of the Matrix.

In this chapter, however, we will examine the 'nature' of the Matrix.

For ordinary people, like you and me, the proof of this holistic universe, this matrix, is to be found within the everyday things that we've been taught to ignore.

In this chapter I will demonstrate that your life extends beyond the confines of your body and indeed this life. I will show that all life is connected within a web of mutually supportive and highly profound relationships.

I will suggest that the holistic universe is a self-regulating system in the process of constant evolution.

IS YOUR MIND IN YOUR BRAIN?

If an alien dissected the eye of a human being, they would conclude that we see things upside down and back to front because indeed we do!

Johannes Kepler figured out, in the seventeenth century, that despite the fact that our eyes are wired wrong we manage to see the world as it is. Well, sort of!

Here's a question! Do you see the world in a little projection room in your head or do you project what you see out into the world?

For decades, scientists have been poking around in people's heads trying to find the bit that houses our internal projection room but they've never been able to find it. This idea, that the world we see is actually **'out-there'** rather than in our heads, is thousands of years old and is called the extramission theory (1).

Professor Rupert Sheldrake in his book, 'The Science Delusion', suggests that our outward projection of visual image is both psychological and physical. Certainly it is true that blind people can actually see things in ways we can't explain. Sharks 'see' using electricity, it would be interesting to know if they see the world as we do?

When I was young I trained as a boilermaker and coded welder. Electric arc light burnt holes in my retina but despite having 'blind spots' I continue to see a complete picture of the world.

The world I see is NOT a direct product of the information my eyes produce but an extrapolation my mind creates and I'm not alone.

Most of us instinctively 'feel' that our vision is 'out there' and not playing in our heads. If I asked you where this book was would you point to your own head or toward your hands?

Sheldrake suggests that we, like all animals, 'see' using perceptual fields. Other animals see using fields projected beyond their bodies that include sound and electricity as well as light. Think of whales, dolphins, sharks, electric eels, birds and bats.

WHAT IS A BRAIN?

In the same book, Professor Sheldrake details the findings of the British Neurologist John Lorber; he found that people who have suffered from Hydrocephalus (water on the brain) as children often live perfectly normal lives despite having serious brain damage. He found sixty people who had 95% of their cranial cavity filled with cerebrospinal fluid. Many had IQs over 100. One young man had an IQ of 126 and a first-class degree in Mathematics but had virtually no brain (2). All he had was a thin layer of brain cells about a millimetre thick. Obviously this lends weight to the idea that the brain is like a television set. All of your memories, your thoughts, hopes and dreams are the programmes that exist in the 'air'. The television, or your brain in this case, is only the transducer of those signals.

It is for this reason that scientist have failed to locate 'memories' in our physical brains. Of course you could take your television and remove a transistor and then when the picture disappears publish a scientific paper explaining that television pictures are contained within your transistor but you would be wrong.

We can laugh at this analogy but that is exactly what 'scientists' are doing when they cut out parts of monkey's brains and tell us that they understand how our minds work.

BOUNCERS AND STORE DETECTIVES

Given that the EM Rope hypothesis suggests that light is bi-directional, it should come as no surprise that vision appears to travel in both directions. If you've ever worked in security you will know that people can feel it when you stare at them. One of the first things I learnt, as a bouncer, was that if you are following anyone, or approaching someone to restrain them, don't look at them directly. Invariably, new members of staff would break this rule and would often get punched in the face; they tended to learn very quickly after that not to look at their target directly.

Animals often wake up if you stare at them. It also happens in reverse. Our dog, Booboo, has the family well trained. When she wants a hotdog, her stare would cut through diamonds.

So if we can sense it when someone stares at us with intent, how is that happening? We must be connected in ways we don't understand.

SAY HELLO AND WAVE GOODBYE

Everyone has had the experience of thinking of someone precisely at the moment that they telephone or email. It's so universal that we hardly bother to mention it anymore, so it seems strange that it is a phenomenon that most scientists dismiss. If you even mention it to Richard Dawkins he would probably have a panic attack and have to breathe into a paper bag.

Unlike Dawkins, Professor Rupert Sheldrake is an old school scientist that tends to follow the evidence to a conclusion rather than the reverse. He has been conducting experiments to prove, what a lot of independent scientists have suspected, that our minds are not contained within our brain but are connected by what he calls, 'Morphic Resonance'.

Sheldrake runs a series of ongoing experiments open to the general public. One tests for the ability to know who is telephoning you and the other is a test to see if you can tell when someone is staring at you.

So far the evidence confirms, what most of us have experienced for ourselves, that our minds are directly connected to the people we care about. When the tests are run for people who are strangers the results are around the level that we would expect for chance.

A BLIND BOY SEES WITH HIS MOTHER'S EYES

Professor Sheldrake mentions a great example of our connections to each other.

E. G. Recordon, an ophthalmologist, had a young boy as a patient who was severely disabled, mentally retarded and almost blind. Strangely, in routine tests he seemed to be able to read letters perfectly well. It turned out that the boy could only read the letters that his mother could see.

Peters and Recordon, eliminated the possibility that the boy was picking up visual or audible signals, first by using screens to separate the boy from the mother and then by distance while carrying out the experiments by telephone.

In the trials there would have been a 3.8% chance of the boy guessing correctly. The boy guessed correctly 38% of the time. The odds of producing this result by chance are billions to one. Obviously, natural telepathy was enhanced in this case by the depth of the mother's love and the child's need.

PSYCHIC DOGS

One notable experiment completed by Professor Sheldrake detailed the story of Jaytee, a dog that always knew when his owner was coming home. Professor Sheldrake conducted strict experiments that ruled out routine, chance and habit. His own experiments were replicated by a team from Austria and was filmed by them. The evidence conclusively showed that Jaytee reacted to his owner's intention to return home irrespective of distance. At the very moment that Jaytee's owner decided to return home Jaytee was filmed becoming alert and going to sit at the window despite the fact that the owner was miles away.

This was largely ignored by the British state controlled media.

When Richard Wiseman tried to debunk the experiment on Paul Mckenna's British TV show he had to falsify the evidence. Despite the fact that Wiseman's results were skewed, the British Media ran with stories slandering Sheldrake and Jaytee.

You have to ask yourself, 'Why?' 'What are they so afraid of?'

CLEVER RATS

Professor Sheldrake's morphic resonance hypothesis predicts that if one member of a genus learns a trick then it should make it easier for all other members of that genus to learn the same trick.

As it turns out, that is exactly what the statistics show. When one kind of rat learns to navigate a particular maze in Oslo, it was shown that the same kind of rats all over the world are suddenly able to navigate the same maze much quicker than the initial test subjects.

This hypothesis has been extensively tested with many different kinds of animal. It has also been shown to work with humans solving a visual puzzle.

STARLINGS DANCE

Have you ever seen starlings dance before they go to bed? Starling Mururation is a phenomenon that has baffled scientists for years. But at this point, the confusion of scientist won't come as much of a surprise!

Scientists have suggested that they dance for warmth but that suggestion is risible. Another reason posited is that they fly as a way to attract friends but this ignores the fact that their singing carries for miles, so the exercise would be pointless.

In my own opinion, I suspect that they fly just for the joy of being able to fly.

What is obvious is that starlings, when they dance, are no longer thinking like individuals. They are obviously a part of their group morphic field. Professor Rupert Sheldrake has demonstrated that starlings react far too quickly for physical senses to process the information.

MORPHIC RESONANCE

It is important that your worldview is rooted in the reality that you see around you, rather than some New Age fantasy. With that in mind, I've presented the previous examples, of a more holistic worldview, before I gave you a technical summary of Professor Sheldrake's theory.

If you've ever swum in the ocean, you might have noticed areas of warm water called 'thermoclines'? You may have noticed areas of salty water called 'haloclines'. This will give you some idea of a 'morphic field'. Imagine an area within an infinite sea that is separate and at the same time a part of the whole.

In order to explain the theory of morphic resonance, I will try to paraphrase from Professor Sheldrake's book, *'Morphic Resonance: the Nature of Formative Causation'*.

1. A morphic field is a self-organising system of nested hierarchies or morphic units. At each level, the whole is more than the sum of the parts and these parts themselves are wholes made up of parts.

2. The wholeness of each level depends on an organising field. This field is within and around the system it organises and is a vibratory pattern of activity that interacts with electromagnetic and quantum fields of the system.

The generic name 'morphic field' includes

◊ (a) morphogenetic fields that shape the development of plants and animals.

◊ (b) Behavioural and perceptual fields that organise the movements, fixed-action patterns and instincts of animals.

◊ (c) Social fields that link together and co-ordinate the behaviour of social groups.

◊   (d) Mental fields that underlie mental activities and shape the habits of minds.

3. Morphic fields contain attractors (goals) that guide a system toward its end state (3)

4. Morphic fields contain the sum of group memory.

MORPHIC RESONANT FIELDS

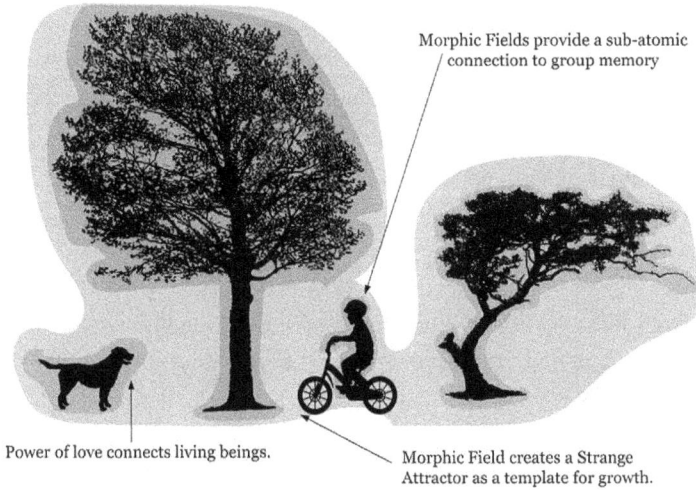

Morphic Fields provide a sub-atomic connection to group memory

Power of love connects living beings.

Morphic Field creates a Strange Attractor as a template for growth.

[Image 18: Individual and group resonant fields.]

WHAT DOES THIS ALL MEAN?

Once we throw off the straight jacket that the religion of materialism has put on science, we find that so much of the world is not the way our 'masters' would have us believe it is!

We are not separate, we are connected to each other and to every living thing in the universe. Through cosmic radiation, which affects our weather, we are connected to the sun, the moon and the stars.

Morphic resonance demonstrates that life is far too complicated to be accidental. The entire universe has had to co-operate in order to create each moment of your life.

It seems only logical that we begin to approach that life with a sense of awe and gratitude. It is that sense of 'sacredness' that materialism has denied us for so long.

THE REALITY OF LIFE BEYOND DEATH

In the book *'Evidence of the Afterlife'* the author, Jeffrey Long MD, details a story of Maria who was rushed into hospital with a severe heart attack. Luckily, she was successfully resuscitated. When she woke up she told Kimberly Clark Sharp that she had left her body and had gone outside of the hospital. She had observed a tennis shoe on the third-storey window ledge. She gave detailed information saying that it was left footed and dark blue. Sharp investigated and did indeed find the tennis shoe where Maria said it was.

Pim Van Lommel MD published a case in the Lancet, one of the world's most prestigious medical journals. A patient suffered a cardiac arrest and was not breathing. When the crash team tried to ventilate him they found that he was wearing dentures. They removed them and placed them in the crash cart draw. A week later, after being saved, he awoke and when the nurse told him that they'd lost his dentures he told her where to look.

Obviously, in both of these examples neither patient could have possibly known the details that they reported unless they had indeed witnessed them while existing outside of their bodies.

It is quite easy for anyone these days to research these things for themselves so I will not bore you with more evidence.

I would, however, like to point out a few points that have occurred to me over the years of researching the nature of the Matrix in regard to 'Out of Body Experiences' (OBE): These points are also confirmed by Jeffrey Long MD.

- The level of consciousness reliably reported at the point of death or after it, is usually exponentially clearer than the normal level of consciousness.

- Physical experiences are often confirmed and occur under general anaesthesia when consciousness should be impossible.

- Near-death experiences are remarkably consistent all over the world irrespective of culture or time.

THE REALITY OF REINCARNATION

It is often helpful to imagine that the body is the physical expression of the individual morphic field. It is not so much that we, as physical bodies, have a 'soul' it is rather that we, as beings of energy, have 'bodies'.

The scars, memories and loves of one life can often be passed on to the new life.

A neat example of this is Jenny Cockell, whose story was reported on the BBC just before her book '*Yesterday's Children*' was published (4).

As a four year old in England, Cockell remembered being Mary Sutton in Ireland. She lived in the town of Malahide and died when she was thirty-five years old after having eight children. She was able to trace her lost children and was able to confirm details of their lives that no living person could have known other than her children.

It is important to note that the evidence does not point to a 'person' being exactly reincarnated as a carbon copy. It appears that we are more like a wave of energy in the ocean. The water does not actually move, it is just the energy that rolls beneath the surface of the water, which gives the impression of a unique wave.

Imagine getting a long rope laid out in front of you and quickly lifting it and pulling it down in a snap. The energy wave passes quickly away from you while the rope never leaves your hand. The evidence suggests that we are like that energy wave, a consciousness continuum, rather than a separate specific identity.

A survey published in 2009 by Theos showed that 53% of the world's population believe in reincarnation and 70% believe in the soul.

Another interesting example is Patrick Christenson who was born in March 1991. His elder brother Kevin had sadly died of cancer twelve years earlier at the age of two. Kevin's cancer was found six months prior to his death. After a fall broke his leg the doctors investigated a swelling behind his right ear. It transpired that the boy had tumours that pushed his left eye forward and caused blindness. He was operated on and was left with a scar on the right side of his neck. Soon after that he died. Twelve years later when Patrick was born he had a birthmark that looked like a cut on the right side of his neck. He also had a nodule on his scalp above the right ear and he had a clouding of his left eye.

When he eventually started to walk he had a limp. He also had clear memories of his life as Kevin.

This would suggest that the morphic field of the living being carries the memories of our past lives. In cases where that connection is strong it is possible for physical characteristics to be passed on.

THE REALITY OF YOUR AURA

An easy way that you can prove to yourself that you are an energy field that has a body is to just have a look at your aura. We are all born with the ability to see auras; it's just that, as we grow up, we learn not to. All you have to do is unlearn that inhibition.

The aura appears transparent at first. It's a bit like looking down a long desert road and seeing the heat shimmer off the tarmac. Auras are like that, transparent disturbances in the air around an object.

Put your hand up with a plain white background behind it and softly stare between your fingers but try not to look at the fingers. After a few moments you will see a clear energy shimmer around your fingers. If you can resist blinking you will very quickly see a light blue sheen emanating from the ends of your fingers.

Often after conducting this experiment, people don't want to believe the evidence of their own senses. They will deny their own observations and defer to a 'scientist'. Of course the scientist will tell you that it is an optical illusion and you will quickly forget about your experiment. Luckily, not all scientists work for the consensus. Russia has a more holistic approach to science, which is a bit ironic considering that it is the home of Marxism.

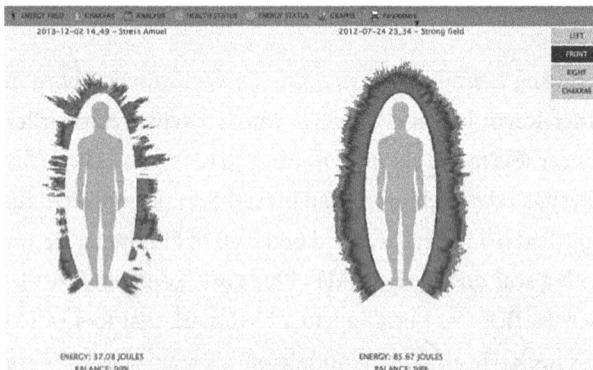

[Image 19: GDV clinical diagnostic image.]

Dr Konstantin Korotkov has produced the Gas Discharge Visualization (GDV) technique, also known as the Electrophotonic Imaging (EPI) System. This system has been available for the last twenty years.

The GDV system is regularly used in diagnosing cancer and is indeed used as a long-term diagnostic tool. The EPI system has been approved by the Russian Health

Authorities for general use, following clinical trials and the recommendation of the Russian Academy of Sciences.

The images it produces suggests the dandelion effect that we would expect to see generated by millions and millions of EM Ropes connecting all the atoms of the body to all the atoms in the universe.

Changes in that field around the body are interpreted by the EPI machine.

Images of human energy fields generated by the EPI system are almost exactly the same as the images of two gold atoms published by the Relativistic Heavy Ion Collider:

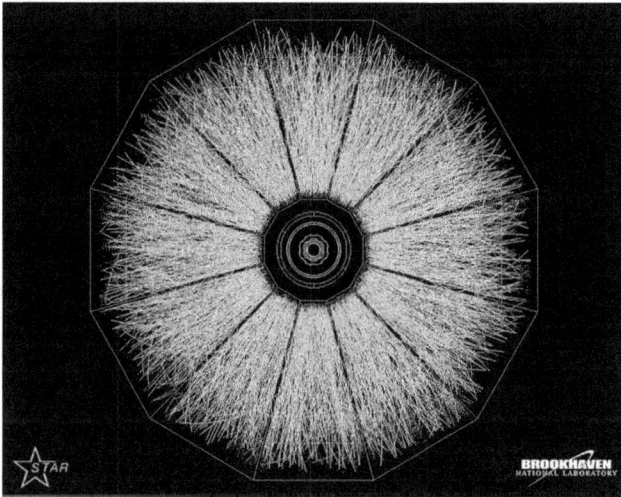

[Image 20: Photo of gold atom from Brookhaven.]

UNITY WITH THE MATRIX

It was originally thought that the form that a living being takes is determined by its DNA but we now know that this is not true.

Professor Sheldrake's hypothesis suggests that form is determined by strange attractors within the morphic field of the subject (see chapter 10 for explanation). We naturally grow towards our own evolution within the template of our morphic field.

This might explain how the process of rapid adaptation is communicated within a morphic group due to environmental stimulus. What is interesting is the perfection towards which we grow and the perfection of that form.

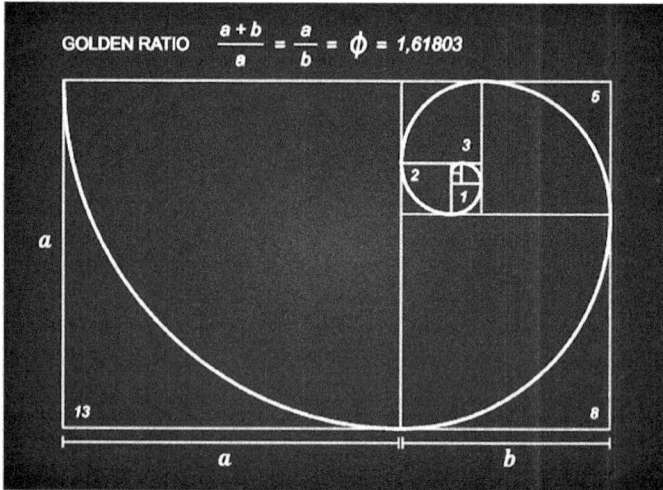

[Image 21: Fibonacci sequence perfection of form.]

Have you ever seen an ugly tree? I used to study photography and my Art Tutor let me into a secret, 'There's no such thing as an ugly tree from the point of view of form.'

The Fibonacci sequence reveals, for our logical minds, what nature has always known: the world around us is perfect. The Fibonacci sequence of numbers are all equal to the sum of the previous two and provide us with the 'Golden Ratio' of 1.61538.

The sunflower, rotating galaxies, the pine cone, the seashell, our DNA, the electromagnetic ropes that connect us to the universe, all contain the same perfection of form.

This perfection of form is just the tip of the iceberg. We can now see that the reality around us is just the physical manifestation of a metaphysical ocean that animates, nurtures and inspires us toward a future in which we all play a vital role.

DO TREES TALK?

Dr Suzanne Simard is a professor with the UBC Faculty of Forestry and she has shown that trees and plants have access to their own internet (5). Plants have a symbiotic relationship with mycorrhizai fungi. Fungi forms an underground system through which trees and plants form a network whereby they share carbon, information, nutrition and water.

Contrary to expectation this system demonstrates that the forest is not competing for resources as natural selection would predict. The facts appear to support the idea that old trees form a hub that supports the life of the forest around it.

It would seem that the Native American Indians and the Celtic Tribes were entirely correct when they understood the forests and the world around them was alive in ways that we are only now beginning to discover.

WHY DOES THIS MATTER?

Our bodies are made of the fabric of this planet whose atoms came from other long dead stars. We live within an eternal and infinite sea of light and dance like waves over the ocean of time and yet we have been convinced by pygmies to believe that we are alone in a meaningless world and that our lives are an accident.

The suffering, that splinter in our mind, is the deeply repressed memory of who and what we really are. It's no wonder that 70% of Americans are on some kind of drug. It's no wonder that so many young people kill themselves.

Everything sacred and wonderful has been sucked out of life by grey people with clip-on ties and entirely pointless white lab coats. Bill Nye even makes me want to kill myself!

ARRIVAL IN LONDON

My wife had forgiven my selfishness and I made my connection in good time.

I'd slept through the flight and was still half-asleep when I got off the plane in London.

The queue for passport control had not moved in half an hour. A middle-class family from Notting Hill were ahead of me by about three hundred people but in our snaking line that put them almost directly in front of me.

They had three small children, two of which were doing a great impersonation of drug addicts high on PCP. They had reluctantly given up trying to hang each other with the security barrier when a security guard asked the parents to keep their children with them. Both parents looked offended by the idea.

We all enjoyed a temporary lull while their emaciated mother fed her children yet more sugar.

The effect was something like snorting three lines of pink champagne: immediate and remarkable. Tarquin and Hugo were now making a good job of beating each other to death with their parent's inflatable flight cushions. I had thought that the poor woman was deformed but about an hour into our sentence, I had realised that Notting Hill woman was wearing a small child like a fashion accessory strapped to her body by 20 feet of what looked like a pashmina.

"Anyone wiv a biometric passport follow me!" A woman wearing a high viz vest shouted and held her clipboard over her head.

Like a greyhound on crack cocaine, Notting Hill man suddenly sprang into life as he shot toward the clear area in front of the empty biometric booths.

He was wearing a Palestinian Keffiyeh and a baseball cap but I don't think he was prepared for armed resistance against the IDF. His jeans were the kind that has the crutch somewhere around the knees.

By making very rapid, but necessarily very short, steps and pushing two old ladies out of his way he managed to drag his wife toward freedom.

Unfortunately, he didn't have time to notice that Tarquin and Hugo were still locked in armed combat. He overcome his impeded agility by virtue of his single-minded determination. Notting Hill man and his wife arrived at the biometric booths ahead of high viz woman and looked around proudly. At least five hundred people were now fighting their way to join them.

From being a passive and resigned group of people, they had become a fighting mob in seconds. Relieved of so many people, our queue started to move forward. Tarquin and Hugo were now looking around for their parents. Hugo began to cry loudly. I could still hear the screaming as I made my way toward baggage reclaim.

CHAPTER 9

****

THE HOLISTIC UNIVERSE

The last time that I'd arrived at Gatwick my offshore project had been cancelled. Yet another helicopter had crashed and as usual all the helicopters in the North Sea were grounded.

They say that human beings now have a concentration span less than a goldfish. That certainly is true of the Health and Safety Executive (HSE) in the UK. Their standard response to any crash in the North Sea would be funny if it wasn't so tragic:

1. Enforce an entirely pointless knee-jerk reaction (like grounding perfectly healthy helicopters). This demonstrates to the public the 'authority' and the 'competence' of the HSE.

2. Wait long enough for the public to forget about the faces of the dead in the newspaper. (These days that can be as little as twenty-four hours.)

3. Carry on as normal.

4. Invent a new 'safety' course for offshore workers to attend. (This used to be called 'abdication of responsibility'.)

After the Piper Alpha disaster and all of these years, it is evident that the government and the HSE serve the oil companies, not the people.

Helicopters are noisy, smelly and very uncomfortable and, in the North Sea, they also have a worrying habit of crashing.

There are two things that you won't find in a helicopter with engine problems: parachutes or atheists! Offshore, there are some things you can discuss and there are some topics that will find you on the 'Not Required Back' list.

Offshore workers have a very limited range of emotional responses. Their response to the words 'God' and 'Paedophilia' are so similar as to be practically indistinguishable. In this modern world, atheism is, to all intents and purposes, state enforced.

Many years ago, I was on the way home and sharing a small helicopter with some rather large men.

These were the sort of men that the British Army have been using as shock troops for hundreds of years. They didn't so much speak as growl. They were practical men, most of whom had a background in engineering and science, all of them were atheists.

Fifty nautical miles from nowhere, a loud bang woke everyone up. The helicopter lurched to port like a wounded deer. The cabin started to fill with smoke.

I looked at the faces of my friends, all of them were praying now!

'Oh! Jesus! Oh! Jesus', I heard from the giant of a man next to me.

I could see the lips of the man opposite me working frantically on a prayer of which he could only remember one line. I could just make out, 'Sweet mother of God'.

So if, when push comes to shove, we all instinctively feel that there is some power, some 'thing' more than us, why is it that atheism is the fastest growing religion in the West?

ABUSIVE RELIGION

I suspect that there are many reasons why so many people in the West call themselves 'atheists', but one of the main reasons has got to be the fact that all organised religions have, in one way or another, betrayed the people they profess to serve.

Here in Spain, the Catholic Church is treated a bit like you would treat that slimy uncle that sexually abused you when you were small: still a part of the family but nobody trusts him with the kids.

In Spain, even the smallest village and hamlet has a huge church or cathedral. It's not hard to see where all the money from the Americas went. At the same time that the bishops were building monuments to their own power, eighty percent of the Spanish people were peasants and effectively kept as slaves in their own country.

The Church and the State grew fat as a once proud people starved.

The Church aggressively resisted any attempt at land reform (1).

WHY DO WE ALL AGREE THIS IS EVIL?

Why is it that we all instinctively know that this abuse of trust is morally and spiritually wrong? How do we all know that the government collusion with multinational business is reprehensible?

Why do we have nothing but contempt for the people who are charged with protecting public safety but do nothing because of their own cowardice?

Where do we get our sense of 'right and wrong' and how is it that we instinctively believe in something greater than ourselves?

IS MORALITY IN YOUR DNA?

Darwin implied and Neo-Darwinists insist that human morality is a product of natural selection. Indeed, we have been brainwashed into the assumption that our morality evolved by accident and is passed on through our DNA (2).

There are many problems with this hypothesis, four of the most obvious howlers I list below:

For Darwin's theory on morality to be true:

- He would have to show evidence of the organism prior to the accidental mutation of 'morality'.

- He would have to show evidence of a transitional form of morality in social structures.

- He would have to show that there was a direct evolutionary advantage to the specific mutated individual.

- He would have to demonstrate that morality is an inheritable trait.

HIS NAME WAS BRIAN

To illustrate how ridiculous this idea is let me take you back hundreds of thousands of years. You are a primitive human living at a time before social groups; co-operation or communication had accidentally mutated themselves into existence.

You are born with a feeling of empathy due to an aberration in the chemical balance in your tiny brain and your name is Brian.

Unlike the rest of your kind you do not desire to rape and kill your way to evolutionary success. You feel that it would be a good idea if everyone could just get along!

In such an environment, it is extremely unlikely that such an individual would survive long enough to mate. Assuming that, by some miracle, our friend Brian lived beyond puberty (although we must remember that Darwin abolished the idea of miracles) can you imagine how he could possibly persuade other proto-humans to co-operate with him? Do you think that he would be able to convince a female to willingly mate with him? The whole idea is beyond satire.

Brian would be dead faster than you can say, 'Can't we just talk about this?'

The truth is that all the available evidence points to the fact that humans have always been a social animal. But this leads me to the last problem: morality is not a physically inherited characteristic.

IF MORALITY IS IN YOUR DNA CAN YOU POINT TO IT?

We now know that DNA is just a sequence of proteins.

You have the same DNA in your arm as you do in your leg. DNA are the building blocks of you. DNA doesn't store the plan of where those blocks go or what they do when they get there.

Science is only now beginning to realise the complexity of DNA, but at the same time we are beginning to see the limitations of it. It was hoped that DNA would contain all the information for life but after decades of research and billions of dollars in investments, the human genome project has produced very little.

DNA is not the 'master plan' or the 'supercomputer' that Bill Clinton sold it as. In fact, DNA is the organism's servant not the master (3).

"In actual fact, human beings live in symbiosis with micro-biota of many hundreds of micro-organisms. The micro-biota are essential to human health and the phenotype of the individual is greatly influenced by interactions with the micro-biota.

The body houses many fold more DNA of microbial origin than it does the genomic DNA inherited from the parents. The individual human is therefore an ecosystem of diverse cellular origins."

(Genetics as an explanation: limits to the Human Genome Project - Irun R Cohen et al)

So if we don't get our sense of morality from natural selection or DNA is it just cultural programming?

Contrary to the popular materialist view, no! This is not the case and it's easy to prove!

QUESTION:

"A healthy man walks into a hospital where five patients are waiting for organ transplants. Is it morally acceptable to kill the man in order to harvest his organs in order to save the lives of the five others?"

If you instantly answered, 'NO!' then you share a near universal response to the dilemma and it's a response shared by peoples and cultures all over the world. In fact, the evidence now suggests that most animals share that same sense of morality.

Therefore, if morality is universal and shared with other animals we would have to say that morality is not a cultural construct and neither is it a physically inherited trait.

WHAT IS MORALITY ANYWAY?

Before we get too excited and take this discussion any further we should pause for a moment in order to agree on what exactly we mean when we say, 'morality'.

I'm going to be quoting extensively from Professor Marc Bekoff's work so I will use his definition here. '*We define morality as a suite of interrelated other-regarding behaviours that cultivate and regulate complex interactions within social groups.*'

Bekoff defines three main categories of 'moral' behaviours and calls them 'clusters'.

- *The Co-operation Cluster.*
- *The Empathy Cluster.*
- *The Justice Cluster.*

The *Co-operation Cluster* consists of altruism, reciprocity, trust, punishment and revenge.

The *Empathy Cluster* consists of sympathy, compassion, caring, helping, grieving and consoling.

The *Justice Cluster* consists of a sense of fair play, sharing, a desire for equity, expectations about what one deserves and how one ought to be treated, indignation, retribution and spite.

(Taken from *'Wild Justice: The Moral Lives of Animals'*. Bekoff and Pierce.)

CLEVER MONKEY

A lot of work has been done over the last few decades by scientists who specialise in animal behaviour.

It has been shown that most animals are born with a sense of justice and morality.

If you're a wolf then your manners will be those of a wolf but that doesn't mean that you don't have any! It's just that modern humans, until now, have not bothered to try to understand how other species really think. We've spent a lot of time exploiting animals but not a lot of time getting to know them.

Monkeys have their cultural norms and we have ours but we all share the same sense of morality.

This point is so important that it bears repeating:

Morality is innate in most animals INCLUDING HUMANS.

Natural Selection is predicated on the idea that advantageous mutations would be directly passed on to the next generation. Unfortunately, morality in any animal makes it less likely that they would get the opportunity to pass on their own DNA to the next generation.

For example, several monkeys were put in a cage and fed whenever they pushed a button. Later on, scientists wired up one of the monkeys to receive an electric shock every time the button was pushed. The monkeys decided that they would rather starve than shock their friend. Obviously, in the wild this altruistic attitude would get you dead real quick.

If Darwin was right then one would imagine that after millions of years of evolution, all animal life would be entirely self-centred and focussed on successful reproduction with as many partners as possible to the exclusion of all else. Interestingly, these are not the behaviours we find in the wild. They are, however, very common in Hollywood.

TO BE OR NOT TO BE?

Nasty Nick was an olive baboon in the southeast corner of Masai Mara National Reserve in Kenya. In his book, '*A Primate's Memoir*' Stanford University Professor, Robert Sapolsky, told the story of this sociopath of a baboon. Nick was fond of a bit of casual rape, assault and intimidation.

Documented cases of animal cruelty to each other are incredibly rare but the evidence does point to the fact that animals can choose to be good or evil.

I know from my own experiences with our adopted Rottweiler, Booboo, that she chooses how to behave and represses her urge toward aggression just as we do every day.

Anyone who has spent any significant time working with both animals and commercial divers will tell you that there really is no difference between the two groups.

THE DEATH OF HUMAN MORALITY

As we have previously discussed, human society has officially abandoned any idea of a natural moral datum and has replaced morality with 'feelings'.

The problem with using 'feelings' as a moral compass is that they are based on the 'Self of Now'. If you base your moral decisions on the sum of your past, how you feel about that past and on your expectation for the future, you will be lost in the tempest of your temporary emotions.

And here is the vital clue! True empathy and altruism exist BENEATH our emotions. The only explanation for the universal nature of morality is that it exists, along with our memories and our thoughts, within the morphic field of our genus.

WHAT IS THE INHERENT NATURE OF THE MATRIX

We only have to look around at nature to see the perfection of life.

Scientists at the National Space Institute in Denmark have proved that it is the cosmic rays entering the Earth's atmosphere that create our clouds and thus our weather systems (4). When solar flares explode from the sun they deflect the cosmic rays and prevent cloud formation and thus this leads to global warming (5).

Professor Hubert Lamb, director of climate research at the University of East Anglia, said in 1971, *'Climate changes come in cycles determined by astronomical and physical factors. One main cause is the amount of radiation received from the sun'.*

Without this complex system of environmental control all life on Earth would be impossible. We have seen that 'morality' seems to be a part of the morphic resonance of our planet and something that all life is tapped into. These highly suggestive observations would lead us to suspect that, rather than not giving a F##K about us, the universe is actually on our side!

WILD TRUTH

In fact, our observations are quite persuasive when you realise that all the great spiritual leaders in the past obtained their unique spiritual vision during, or after, a prolonged period of time spent in seclusion in the wild.

Buddha spent years alone in the Deer Park sitting under a Bo tree. Jesus was reported as spending long periods alone in the desert. Mohammed spoke to the angel Gabriel in a cave. Baal Shem Tov became one of the greatest teachers of Jewish mysticism alone in the forest.

Throughout history most great spiritual teachers had a strong connection to nature and spent extended periods alone in the wild.

MORAL STRAITJACKET

Organised religions seek to impose their own ideas of what is 'good' and what is 'evil'. Usually a religion's system of morality is entirely a product of the time and culture of its genesis, rather than some universal datum to which we all have access.

At the other end of the spectrum of insanity, in our present Cultural Marxist system, the morality to which you are expected to conform is dependent on which minority group you belong to.

With no clear guidance from the elites and our governments, today, morality is decided on social media. After two thousand years of progress Good and Evil are now, once again, decided by the mob.

The evidence shows that natural morality is something that all living things have access to. It also assumes that any attempt to manipulate the morality of others is bound to fail.

Therefore, as we are all connected to the one Matrix, the only morality that you need to be concerned with is your own and the datum by which you judge yourself is the silent voice within, which is the Matrix itself.

In effect, this produces a harder datum to follow because we are all aware of our own inner life.

WHY THIS ALL MATTERS?

As a summary then we can say that, contrary to materialist philosophy, the very essence of the universe is 'goodness' itself. Beyond all probability or chance, every day of our lives we are supported by an infinite universe whose very nature is what we call 'selfless love'.

Contrary to Darwin's depressing view of life, the forests, the plants and the animals all conspire to aid each other in a connected and interdependent world.

Our own personal morality is a natural expression of that universal love and awareness.

When we learn to go beneath the 'Self of Now' we find that our deepest essence is also that same clear lake of love that is the essence of the Holistic Universe.

We could also go further and conclude that any attempt to enshrine morality or spiritual understanding in a book would condemn the seeker to magnify their own sense of the 'Self of Now'. Experiential wisdom cannot be contained within a book. It must be arrived at through experience.

The universe has no need of books on which to record its truth, because it is already written on our very essence.

GATWICK ARRIVALS

The LCD overhead told me that my bags will arrive on line 2. I managed to grab a trolley and made my way over to the belt.

As I positioned myself for a clear view of the incoming luggage, I found people trying to push in front of me. As the crowd pushed in on me, I could feel my tiredness push my anger toward my heart like a rising wave. I could feel the people around me tense.

The gentleman from Nigeria, who had spent the entire flight kicking the back of my seat, now tried to push his trolley in front of mine. As the 'red mist' descended, my body prepared itself for combat.

I took a deep breath and let the wave rush over me. I neither pushed it away nor tried to justify it. I pushed my mind toward the essence of the Matrix that unites us.

I felt my body relax. I'd beaten my murderous nature once again. As if a cloud had passed, the people around me relaxed.

The Nigerian gentleman turned to me and smiled, "Sorry didn't mean to be rude! I'm so excited to see my wife! I feel like a boy again!"

I couldn't help laughing. I pulled my trolley back to allow him to pass.

How wonderful life is!

"How long have you been apart?" I asked with a smile.

****

CHAPTER 10

THE SECRET OF DARK MATTER

My connection to Aberdeen had been booked for 07:00 hours the next day, so I was to be marooned at Gatwick for the night. I didn't mind, I've had to overnight in worse places and, if I'm honest, I quite like Gatwick.

Over the years, the Sofitel Hotel had become a home-from-home.

In the restaurant, later that evening, I was just trying to find something new to eat on the menu, when a shadow appeared at my elbow. I looked up to see a smartly dressed, middle-aged women smiling down at me.

"Antonio?" She said with an accent as precise as Porsche engineering. She had the polish of money but lacked the matey condescension of the police. I frowned, expecting a lawyer.

"Antonio Sebastian?" She said, hopefully. "My God! You bastard! You don't remember me do you?"

Concluding that only the people who know me well tend to call me 'bastard', I relaxed.

"I'm terribly sorry! Won't you sit down and remind me!"

I half stood and indicated the other side of the table.

"Vicci! Vicci Wokmann," she said, now sounding hurt.

I felt mortified. I couldn't believe it. In what seemed like another lifetime, I had met and loved a young BA air hostess named Vicci. To the young commercial diver from a desperately poor background, she had seemed more perfect than real.

If I ever get around to writing a story about an English princess, I would have to cast Vicci, well the Vicci of my memory, to play the part.

She had been one of the last real English débutantes and never tired of pointing out the difference in our backgrounds. She had loved ballet and I had just loved her. In the end that just wasn't enough for Vicci.

She had always reminded me of the line from Tom Robinson's song 'War Baby', **_"Only the very young and the very beautiful can be so aloof."_**

I squinted to try to see that young girl within the woman who now claimed her name. The light that had burned so bright, so long ago, had become something else, something gentler, sadder and perhaps infinitely kinder.

"Oh God! Have I changed that much? You look like someone trying to figure out the cryptic crossword in the Sunday Times."

"Are you working?" I asked hoping to deflect her attention from the obvious disaster that was our mutual age.

She held my eye a little too long and smiled sadly. "Why do we take our youth for granted?" She whispered and shook her head.

As it turned out, Vicci was due to run BA's first flight to Delhi in the morning. Dinner was the least I could do for the old enemy buried within this friendly stranger.

When she laughed I could just about recognise the girl I had once loved. I decided that I actually liked this Vicci a lot more than the first.

Dinner had been jolly but by the time dessert arrived she seemed frosty again. The silences got longer.

"I'm sorry, if I hurt you," she offered hopefully, not looking me in the eye.

I shrugged, "That was a long time ago!" But we both knew that it wasn't.

She glanced behind her at two Arab gentlemen, I realised now that they had indeed been staring at her all evening. She looked embarrassed.

"Are you OK? Do you know them?" I asked.

"No! I could just feel them staring at me! Even after all these years it makes me feel uncomfortable."

"They're probably betting that they've seen you before but can't remember where."

"I can always tell when someone is just admiring and I can tell when someone has bad intentions," She said in a small voice.

I signalled to the waiter and called for the bill.

"Come on I'll walk you to your room. Forget about them for tonight."

As I left Vicci and her door closed, I wondered if it were possible that our actions create an energy that leads to the accidents and coincidences of our busy lives. All those years ago, it was Vicci's rejection of me based on the circumstances of my birth that nearly destroyed me. Her rejection confirmed the opinion of my sisters, "I would never be good enough simply because I was me."

Now, twenty years later, it seemed that life had conspired to provide Vicci with a mirror of her own youthful arrogance. Could it be that the Holistic Universe seeks balance?

THE GENESIS OF HUMAN SUFFERING

When I was young, in the 1960s, the establishment told us that divorce was a good thing and that children were resilient. That has not proved to be the case, in fact the opposite has proved true.

In the early 1900s, my family, on my father's side, were Sephardic Jews living in Ceylon who had, like many of their race, converted to Catholicism. When my grandfather was wounded whilst fighting in France during the First World War, he fell in love with an English nurse. After the birth of my father, my grandfather and his English wife moved back to Ceylon. After several years, my grandmother inevitably, and somewhat unfortunately for everyone concerned, discovered that her husband was originally Jewish.

Predictably enough, she promptly left her husband, and taking her two young sons, returned to England. You have to understand that between the two world wars, anti-Semitism was effectively compulsory in Europe.

Looking back at the history of my family it is easy to see how every life decision and every action seemed to inevitably cause suffering to roll down through the decades like a snowball down a mountain.

Today a corrosive materialistic worldview encourages us to believe that we live alone and in a vacuum.

The immediate gratification of the individual has become the golden principal of our society. But if you sit down and think about your life you will see that suffering passes down through time and space and affects everyone it touches.

The decisions of my ancestors throughout the 1800s have directly affected my life and the suffering that I've experienced, but that begs the question, "what is this thing we call 'suffering'?"

THE DARK SECRET

The three questions that have boiled everyone's brains for the last three thousand years are these:

1. Does 'suffering' exist separately and externally to me or does it remain within me?

2. Why do some actions cause 'suffering' and others do not?

3. How do we deal with the phenomena of human suffering?

Historically speaking, most of the answers that have been offered have not proved to be very satisfying and there is a very good reason for that! Most of us, for most of the time, look at life all wrong and inevitably our answers are necessarily incomplete.

We tend to look at life as a series of separate events, like polaroids or snap-shots of life. Looking at our earlier example from my own life, we could go back in time and watch my grandmother leave her husband and we might assume that all the subsequent suffering in my own family was caused by this one act by a stupid and selfish woman. Such a simple answer is attractive but it's fundamentally wrong because life isn't a series of snap-shots, it's a movie.

The anti-Semitism that infected my grandmother didn't start with her, it was born two thousand years ago in a war against the Romans and was nurtured with the birth of Christianity. This is the 'dependent origination' of my grandmother's prejudice.

Indeed, her selfishness and arrogance was born out of the women's suffragette movement, which itself was a reaction against centuries of oppression and the social turmoil left behind in the aftermath of the First World War.

No act or event exists in a vacuum; everything is affected by everything else. As we discussed in chapter 2, the Buddha called this process of endless causation, 'dependent origination' and it's a lot like gravity.

Gravity is invisible. It's always there but we don't see it until objects and events reveal its presence. Sir Isaac Newton would not have been able to discuss gravity without seeing an apple fall.

Similarly, my grandmother's prejudice and arrogance had followed her from England to Ceylon like an invisible cloud of negativity until the events of her life were ripe for it to manifest in the world.

From this example, we can conclude that my family's suffering did not begin with my grandmother's actions but were influenced by a wave of negative dependent origination that already existed. So this in turn begs the question, "why do some actions cause an invisible force of 'negative dependent origination' and others do not?"

If you think about your own life for a moment, you will easily see that every intention you have ever had has created dependent origination of one form or another (1).

But what the Buddha failed to notice was that some actions create a *negative dependent origination*, which results in suffering, while other actions seem to create balance and evolution, in other words, *positive dependent origination.*

Looking at my own example, we could say that anti-Semitism is born out of a deep feeling of the 'Self of Now' as being separate to the 'other'. My grandmother's arrogance was obviously born out of her deep sense of her 'Self of Now' as being superior to Jews. When she took her two sons from their father and left Ceylon to return to England she was choosing herself over the world, just as Buddha did when he left his newborn son and his wife.

We can therefore make the assumption that any volition that originates within the illusion of the 'Self of Now' will necessarily cause a wave of negative dependent origination. In order to differentiate this 'wave' of negative dependent origination from our reaction to it, let's call this wave of potential energy, '**Dark Matter**'.

Quantum physics also uses the term 'Dark Matter' to refer to something that cannot be seen but whose existence is revealed by events in the real world.

THEORETICAL PHYSICS NEEDS DARK MATTER:

For astronomers 'Dark Matter' is a concept whose sole purpose is to refer to a motivating force that we cannot see but whose existence is required to explain the observed movements of galaxies. In modern theoretical Physics, 'Dark Matter' is an invisible force the existence of which can only be inferred rather than proved.

In the early twentieth century, Professor Jacobus Kapteyn, a Dutch Astronomer, noticed that the velocity and orbit of many planets and galaxies seems to be motivated by a force we cannot see. The hypothetical source of this motivating force he referred to as 'Dark Matter', borrowing a term used by Henri Poincare (2).

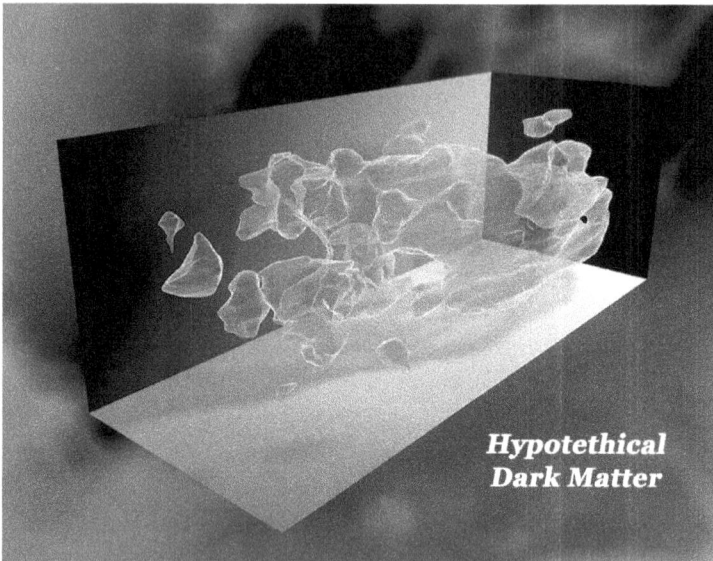

[Image 22: Dark Matter visualisation.]

In the same way, the shape of our fate seems to be moulded by a force we can only conceptualise from the inexplicable events and coincidences of our lives. Like galaxies, our lives move in directions and at speeds that seem, at first, to be random.

If Einstein's universe of separate particles were true, it would be impossible to imagine a mechanism that might create this wave of negative dependent origination but within the Holistic Universe, made up of electromagnetic ropes of light, I was beginning to glimpse a possible explanation.

Thoughts and emotions are expressed in this world as electromagnetic pulses. The question is could those pulses exist beyond the confines of our brain?

HOW COULD DARK MATTER BE CREATED?

You could say that my 'intention' turned toward my idea of my 'Self of Now' causes a form of 'darkness' that can, without physical contact, be sensed by others just as our Arab businessmen made Vicci feel uncomfortable.

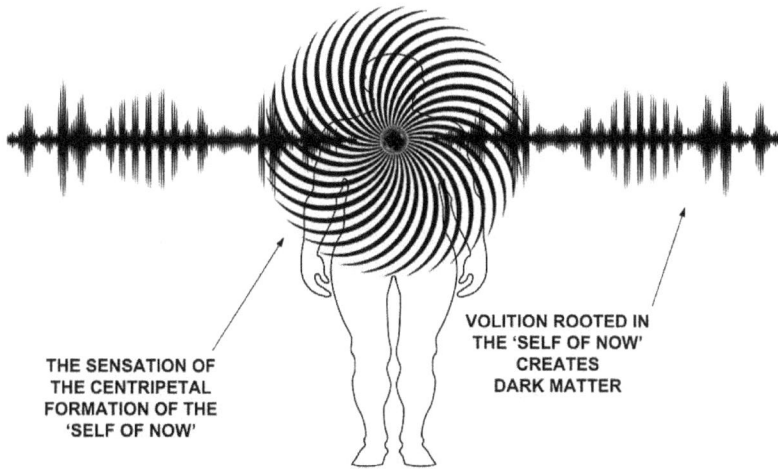

THE SENSATION OF
THE CENTRIPETAL
FORMATION OF THE
'SELF OF NOW'

VOLITION ROOTED IN
THE 'SELF OF NOW'
CREATES
DARK MATTER

[Image 23: 'Self of Now' creates Dark Matter.]

Within the ultrasonics industry the mechanisms by which stresses upon organic objects create electromagnetic energy are well known. In the context of the Holistic Universe it is quite easy to see how 'Dark Matter' might be generated.

Within the petrochemical and power generation industry, for most of my life I have been using advance ultrasonics in order to inspect critical structures. I never realised that ultrasonics might hold the key to understanding the nature of human suffering.

THE PIEZOELECTRIC EFFECT

In 1880, two French physicists named Jacques and Pierre Curie, discovered that an electrical 'charge' gathers in certain materials in response to an applied mechanical stress. Materials like bone, DNA and some proteins, when stressed emit an electrical signal and conversely when exposed to an electrical signal they deform (3).

As our mental processes appear to be entirely made up of electrical signals within an electromagnetic matrix, it does seem possible that our thoughts and intentions do exert an affect in the real world?

PIEZOELECTRICITY

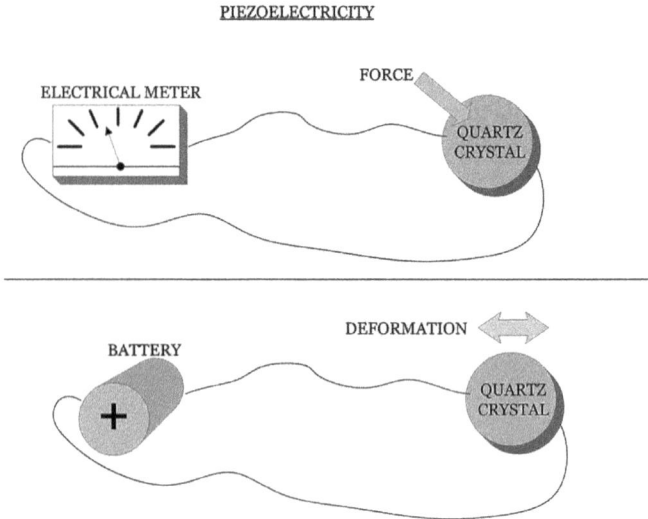

[Image 24: Piezoelectric effect on organic material.]

Research into the effect that mobile phone towers might have on the people living near them has demonstrated that between 10 and 100 hertz (0.3 - 2 Watts per kilogram) human cells appear to be damaged. Electromagnetic waves also cause an increase in the production of yeasts and viruses that may lead to cancer (4).

We can see from these facts that organic material has the potential for creating electromagnetic energy and we have seen that electromagnetic energy has an effect on organic material.

Most societies and cultures, throughout history, have been aware of the negative affect that our intentions can have on other people.

THE EVIL EYE!

Most men love porn! The sexuality of most men is inherently visual and because of that they can often grasp the concept of 'Dark Matter' quite easily because they live with it every day.

It is interesting to note that, throughout history and all over the world, street culture has always warned against this 'negative' energy and the power of the evil eye.

Amulets like the 'Hand of Fatima' were designed to ward of the effects of the 'evil eye' and can still be bought from high-street jewellers today, in one form or another.

Obviously most of these legends are just a mixture of superstition and cultural programming but from the anthropological point of view, the 'evil eye' has its roots in a common human experience.

In most cultures, throughout history, the darkness of our 'evil' intention has been regarded as something real that exists independently in the world 'out there'.

Let's look at two examples:

Self of Now: If I look at a woman through my sense of the 'Self of Now', with the sole intention of enjoying her form for myself, irrespective of how good looking I am or how much money I might have, all things being equal, my stare will elicit a negative reaction from the lady in question. It will make her feel uncomfortable even if she doesn't catch me.

Self of Tomorrow: Conversely, if I forget about my sense of 'self' and look at the woman with an awareness of who that person truly is, with a concern for that person, then usually (all things being equal), I will elicit a positive reaction from the lady in question.

It is evident then that the 'Self of Now' seems to create some kind of 'negativity', a wave that can often be sensed by strangers. Many years ago, I worked as Door Security in some London nightclubs; we often noticed how one person in a group of men, staring intently at a woman, could change the mood of the crowd.

He seemed to invisibly affect the mood of the people that were connected to him. I would often get a poke in the ribs from a colleague and a nod in the man's direction with the comment, 'It's gonna kick off!'

Looking back at my life, it seems to me that 'negativity' breeds 'negativity'.

This would suggest that when my grandmother formed that judgement of my grandfather she may have created a wave of negative dependent origination that we might call 'dark matter' and that negative energy rolled down the decades infecting the lives of everyone who was connected to that morphic field.

THE FORMATION OF THE DARK CRYSTAL
So far we have discussed the ways in which Dark Matter might be created and exist in the 'world out there', but of course, Dark Matter tends to also exist within us.

Most often this Dark Matter, usually through events and interactions with the people around us, can cause distortions in the way that we look at the world. It distorts our ability to interpret the signals that our senses give us.

Most of us have a semi-permanent 'feeling' that exists beneath our emotions that distorts our perception of reality. With practice you will be able to identify the background 'feeling' that forms the prism though which you view the world.

Take Lynda, she had been abandoned by her father, sexually abused and then rejected by her paternal family. Every time Lynda walks into a supermarket she is convinced that everyone is looking at her and judging her.

She becomes erratic and aggressive. She is not seeing life as it is, but rather she is seeing the world through the distortion of her past.

We call the lens though which we see a distorted view of the world the 'Dark Crystal'.

The Dark Crystal is like a perceptual psychological limp that your life has given you.

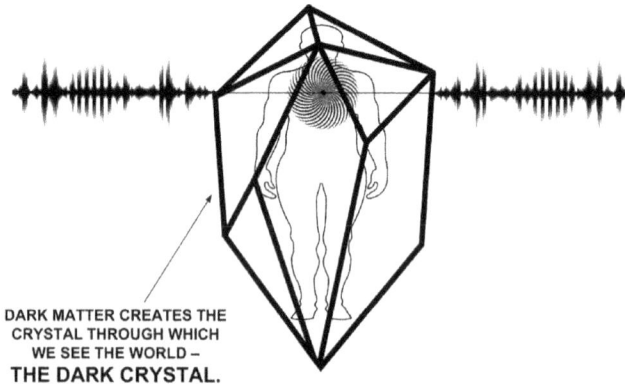

DARK MATTER CREATES THE
CRYSTAL THROUGH WHICH
WE SEE THE WORLD –
THE DARK CRYSTAL.

[Image 25: Formation of Dark Crystal by Dark Matter.]

We have seen that the direction of intention directed at the 'Self of Now' creates a centripetal movement within the mind. We have also seen that without verbal or physical communication that negative centripetal energy can be communicated from one living being to another.

HOW MIGHT DARK MATTER AFFECT THE FUTURE

The big question is how does Dark Matter have a physical affect on our lives. We have looked at possible ways that a potential energy might be created by our volition but how could that potential energy affect changes in our day-to-day life?

To suggest an answer to that question let me explain another important concept: *Chaos Theory.*

Edward Lorenz was a meteorologist and mathematician and he tried to create a computer model to predict the weather. He found that it was impossible to predict complex systems due to micro-changes to initial conditions. For example, imagine that you've made a four-week prediction for the weather in the North Sea. Everything looks great for two days but after that your model is hopelessly wrong. By the time you get to day 28 your model is lost. Any change in initial conditions creates chaotic system divergence.

CHAOS THEORY: STRANGE ATTRACTORS

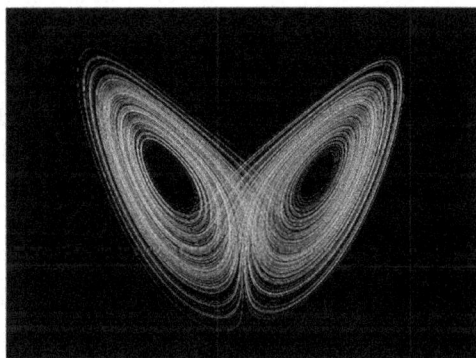

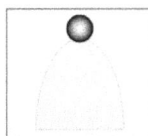

Lorenz Attractor: A

Using gravity as a model.
Unstable System

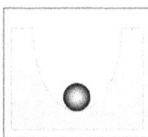

Lorenz Attractor: B

Using gravity as a model.
Stable System

Computer model of Strange Attractors in Chaos system.

[Image 26: Chaos Theory — Strange Attractors.]

What Lorenz found was that just the beating of a butterfly's wings in Kenya might change the initial weather conditions enough to cause a storm in the North Sea (5).

He noticed that individual data points were seemingly drawn to form profoundly harmonious patterns. The cause of this harmony was what came to be called Lorenz Attractors (Strange Attractor).

It seems that the attractor provides a stability in systems that appear to be in chaos. Biologist Conrad Waddington described the goal-directed nature of embryonic development in terms of attractors in an 'epigenetic landscape'.

Professor Sheldrake suggests that all living things are drawn toward their evolution by the strange attractors of their morphic fields.

In order to really conceptualise the action of Dark Matter you could imagine that our actions are like pebbles dropped into a pond. The energy created by our actions causes ripples on the surface of the pond. They spread out toward the walls of the pond and then rebound toward the centre.

That centre point could be considered to be a Strange Attractor.

WHAT IS THE PURPOSE OF DARK MATTER:
In many ways, QM4YS Dark Matter is a much deeper concept than the Indian idea of karma.

It has become fashionable to call any idea of fate or pre-destination, 'karma' but that is to totally misunderstand the concept. Karma is an idea that pre-dates Buddhism and, like socialism, means something different to everyone it meets. However, it is safe to say that in Buddhism karma refers to the process of cause and effect. The doctrine states that if you live a good life then good stuff will happen to you and if not, then you're truly screwed.

If you are a dog being skinned alive by a Vietnamese Buddhist peasant and if you could complain you would be told, with a shrug, that your suffering was the product of your individual karma. This rather fatalistic and nihilistic view of life creates a moral vacuum that has in the past given rise, in Buddhist countries, to some of the world's worst atrocities.

In the Orient, the idea of karma assumes a passive universe. Like our unfortunate dog, we are victims of a totally arbitrary and morally ambivalent universe. Karma is something that is mindlessly done to us in order to maintain an unspecified status quo.

Thankfully, the QM4YS system suggests that the universe might actually have our best interests at heart!

The universe seems to be in a constant state of physical and spiritual evolution toward ever greater perfection and complexity. I would suggest that the Holistic Universe exists like a computer program that is busy writing itself. It would follow that 'suffering' is a built-in feedback loop that pushes the universe toward the Strange Attractor of its own evolution.

Let's look at an example: remember Jeffrey Dahmer? The Milwaukee Cannibal raped, murdered and then ate 17 men and boys.

When he was in prison he became a 'born-again' Christian. Minister Roy Ratcliff baptised Dahmer into the Church of Jesus Christ. The Christian Church celebrated that Dahmer had "***come home to God***" and forgave him his sins in the name of Jesus Christ.

Dahmer's belief in Christ did not bring seventeen people back to life. Nor, did it stop the families of his victims from feeling hate toward him. Dahmer's belief in Christ could not heal the damage in his mind that caused him to kill in the first place. In fact, nothing had changed for Dahmer other than his belief.

In 1994, Dahmer was beaten to death by a fellow inmate.

Obviously all of the events that led to Dahmer's damaged mind, his actions and his life had led him to that one moment of truth when he, himself, was murdered.

The sum of those actions that 'exist' out there in the real world seemed to return and provide Dahmer with a mirror to his own soul.

Just as the wind is invisible until it lifts the leaves and the waves, the Dark Matter that was caused by Dahmer's negative intentions was invisible until it lifted events around Dahmer. Eventually the universe demanded growth. Either Dahmer would evolve as a person or the world around him would change in order to balance the energy that he himself had created.

TURNING DARKNESS INTO LIGHT

In order to find an end to suffering we have examined, in some detail, how it begins. After all, it's only logical that without understanding the beginning of something you would never be able to find its end.

The QM4YS system demonstrates the following points:

- *Dark Matter is a force of negative dependent origination created by any volition focused on the 'Self of Now'.*

- *Dark Matter can be spread like a virus to other living beings.*

- *Dark Matter exists in the world as an invisible force that acts like a Strange Attractor and effects events in the real world.*

- *Dark Matter creates a distortion within us called the Dark Crystal.*

- *The suffering that Dark Matter creates is like a wave that pushes us toward evolution.*

As Dark Matter is, obviously, a fact of life, we have to ask ourselves, 'What can we do about it?'

If we imagine Dark Matter like a weight of water pushing us forward, we could say that at any point in our lives we have the choice to either balance that wave or to allow it to gain momentum and spread suffering through time and space.

As an example, my father had two choices:

1. Make sure that his love and commitment to his wife and children gave them the strength to survive the loss of their country, class and their culture.

2. Focus entirely on himself and get through life as best he could.

My father chose box two and allowed the wave of Dark Matter to gain momentum and power as it spread from life to life through the years. His self-obsession was like a hand-grenade thrown into the centre of our lives.

Similarly, Jeffrey Dahmer and Charles Manson could have decided that they would not allow the Dark Matter, that had damaged their young lives, to damage any one else (6). Conversely, they might have choose to focus entirely on themselves and allow that wave of negative dependent origination to infect the world.

The reason that none of those men decided to re-balance the force of Dark Matter was that they were lost within the illusion of the 'Self of Now'. It follows therefore that in order to do anything about Dark Matter we first have to take control of the 'Self of Now'.

Only when we restrict our automatic reaction can we create a space to redress the balance of Dark Matter.

The universe demands that we change. We have two choices, we can either change by being proactive or we can react to the suffering of life

A big part of ensuring that Dark Matter is neutralised is the process of finding the damage that has been done to our own Dark Crystal. How do you find a way to see what you need to change when you know that we all look at life through the distortions of our own Dark Crystal?

FINDING CLARITY WITHIN THE DARK CRYSTAL

In fact, when we allow ourselves to be quiet and still it becomes obvious that life conspires to provide us with a mirror. Life tells us exactly how to balance the negative energy of Dark Matter through the process of suffering.

As an example, if at anytime my father had been able to be truly present in the moment, he might have seen how he was breaking my mother's heart. He could have used the pain of losing his wife as a wake-up call. We see this process all the time in movies and those stories work because we are all subconsciously aware of the process.

The Holistic Universe provides us with clarity if only we can learn to truly listen to what it is trying to tell us.

As you will see in the next chapter, it was for this reason that the QM4YS system uses a form of Deep Coaching in order to provide a focus and a mirror so that the seeker can find the clarity and strength to overcome the Dark Matter in their lives.

BREAKFAST AT JAIME'S

Check-in opened at 05:00 hours. I got through security and made my way to Jaime Oliver's little restaurant for a spot of breakfast. Two lads wearing the red nylon shirts of Aberdeen Football Club walked in ahead of me. Their kilts were worn, for no explicable reason, with heavy walking boots.

Nylon football shirts always seem to stink of stale sweat no matter how often they're washed so I was glad that they didn't wait for the waitress to seat them. She would have tried to herd us all together in order to save her walking. As she ran after them, I took the time to read the emails on my phone.

Vicci had left for Delhi with the two Arabs on her fight. As it turned out they knew her from the ballet she had seen at Covent Garden the week before.

That was something she and I could never share. I hated ballet with a passion.

The waitress looked like she was suffering from post traumatic stress so I smiled and didn't wait to be chivvied toward the football fans. I sat down by the opposite window. She gave up and took my order.

I was amazed to notice that the two lads were drunk already, or more accurately, still! Out of the corner of my eye, I noticed the hawk faced boy nudge his redheaded friend. Sure enough he swaggered over.

"We no good nough for ya!" he ventured.

This wasn't my first rodeo, so I smiled.

"Mackenzie is it?" I asked.

Red hair looked bemused. The conversation was obviously taking an unexpected turn.

"I was just admiring your kilt. It's the Mackenzie dress tartan is it not?"

Red hair looked down to confirm for himself. When he looked up he was obviously pleased with himself.

"Aye!"

"Did the 'dandies' win?" I ventured.

Warming to the new turn, Red beamed back, "Aye that they did!"

I nodded.

"Great news then, enjoy your breakfast," I turned to my newspaper by way of a dismissal.

He hopped from one foot to the other and then retreated to his friend. I could just hear him dismiss his friends hisses with, "No, he's alright! Leave it!"

CHAPTER II

WHY WE ALL NEED A COACH

When I was young, John Travolta's face was everywhere. Even after all of these years, his face was all over Gatwick airport selling watches.

Mr Travolta has taken a lot of flak for being a scientologist. I always thought that it took a lot of courage to come out and admit to something so silly.

According to L. Ron Hubbard, 75 million years ago, Xenu was the head of a Galactic Federation of 76 planets (1). To deal with overpopulation, Xenu had some of his people killed and frozen. He then ordered a fleet of spaceships, that looked like DC 8 planes, to transport the frozen corpses to Earth in order to blow them up in volcanoes (possibly a slight over reaction!). These poor superfluous citizens who had been killed, frozen, transported, dropped in a volcano and blown up by a hydrogen bomb apparently survived as disembodied souls, called 'Thetans', by attaching themselves to other living beings. Today these Thetans survive by attaching themselves to humans.

Despite Thetans being so determined to live that they survived Xenu's vendetta, apparently these spirits can now be persuaded to leave their human host if asked nicely! As ridiculous as the Scientology backstory is, to be honest, it's no sillier than the narratives that support most religions.

Most of the prominent people involved with the Church of Scientology are incredibly intelligent and successful. Why would anyone in the public gaze subject themselves to public vilification by coming out and admitting that they believe in L. Ron Hubbard's third-rate science fiction nonsense? Looking at these apparently shiny happy people, you would have to say that the reason that they follow Scientology is because, for them, it works!

BECAUSE, FOR SOME PEOPLE, IT DOES WORK!

But it's ridiculous! So how can it possibly work? I hear you scream and I sympathise!

But let's just put that elephant to one side of the room for the moment.

What interested me was Tom Cruise's description of 'Going Clear'.

After years and at least 200,000 dollars (so I'm told) a scientologist might hope to finally get free of the negative spirits (Thetans), which infect his or her body. The programme that one goes through to achieve 'Clear' is a process of frequent auditing sessions. During 'auditing' one is attached to a simple form of lie detector and asked questions to find out where you may have had trauma in one's life.

The rationale behind auditing assumes that by confronting the underlying event that sparked a trauma one can allow the associated Thetan to detach itself from one's body.

What is strange is that this process seems to work for so many people.

WE ALL NEED A MIRROR

We have explored how Dark Matter is created and how it can infect our lives. The problem for all of us is that life is so confusing.

We all long for a connection and more than anything we need some kind of clarity in our lives.

It may be for that reason that human beings, caught up in the chaos of life, have always sought out some kind of third party to provide a kind of mirror, counsellor, priest, or Sharman.

THE ELDERS

A long time ago, when we had huge extended families and the 'Clan' system, people would go to the 'Elders' of the clan for advice and guidance.

The Celts had the Druids. In India they have the Akashwani. The Greeks had Delphi.

The concept of the 'Sharman' is common to nearly all cultures throughout history. Unfortunately, with our 'Me-centred' culture people are now so shallow and disagreeable that we tend to ship old people off to retirement homes as quickly as possible and complain if we have to see them at Christmas.

After a lifetime of thinking very little, it is unlikely that anyone would go to Uncle Chuck in order to unlock the secrets of their soul. His self-obsession would make it impossible for him to connect to the wisdom that is within us all.

ALCOHOLICS

Alcoholics Anonymous (AA) has a great system of mutual support. Group confession and a private relationship with the sponsor has provided a lot of people with the support they needed to turn their lives around and recover from a lifetime of addiction and abuse.

The fundamental cornerstone of AA is to realise that you need the support of other people if you are going to bring 'light' into your life instead of darkness. The realisation that, on our own, we are helpless seems to reduce the power of the 'Self of Now' to manageable proportions.

CATHOLIC CHURCH

Confession was added to the sacraments of the Catholic Church sometime in the sixth century. What could have been hugely helpful to people as a form of one-to-one counselling was negated by a somewhat unrealistic understanding of human psychology. If you assume that someone is 'saved' through accepting a particular belief then you are not really interested in self-development.

The Church quickly gave up even pretending to take the sacrament of confession seriously and almost immediately began selling forgiveness to the highest bidder.

It was this hypocrisy that Martin Luther was reacting against when he posted his declaration on the church door.

THROUGH A GLASS DARKLY

Dark Matter causes pain and suffering in the moment but the damage it does to us is not limited to that specific moment. You may hurt yourself but equally you may be a victim of someone else's darkness. In many ways that trauma can cause mental scars, which then make it impossible for you to see reality clearly.

In the QM4YS system we refer to the semi-permanent 'feeling' that lay beneath the emotions and through which we interpret the world as the 'Dark Crystal'.

In many ways, in the QM4YS system dealing with these 'distortions' in perception is effectively very similar to Scientology's process of 'Going Clear'.

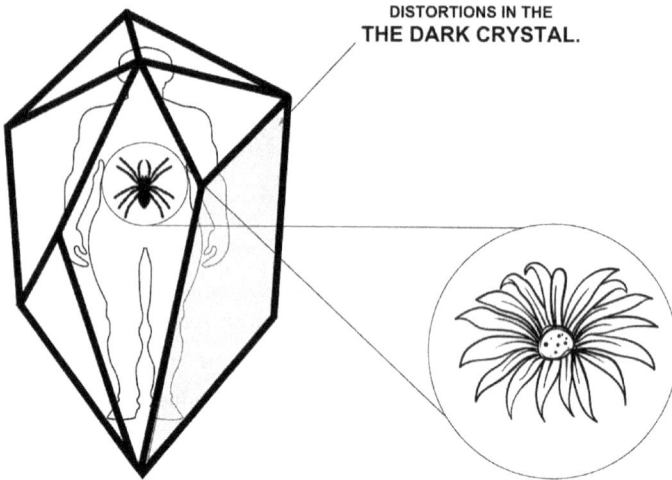

DISTORTIONS IN THE
THE DARK CRYSTAL.

[Image 27: Distortions in the Dark Crystal.]

I've already mentioned my own body dysmorphia so I will give you another example in order to illustrate the distortions in the Dark Crystal:

I learnt at a young age that success and inclusion belonged to other people but never me. My life was lived on the edge of a disintegrating family and I had my existence between the cracks of their lives. They were the ones who had success and respect, never me.

No matter what I ever said or did, it was never going to absolve me of the sin of being me.

In my lifetime, I have been lucky enough to do everything I ever wanted to do. I've travelled the world, literally sailed the Seven Seas and driven across the Sahara Desert. I've been incredibly successful in my offshore career and run multimillion-pound projects. Indeed, I've explored secret caverns that no human had ever seen and swam within the wrecks of long dead ships but none of those things ever made me feel worthy. I never got one bit of joy out of any of those achievements, they never made me feel good enough, thanks to the damage to my Dark Crystal nothing ever could.

MY ANXIETY AND SELF-LOATHING WAS A CLUE.

Through the process of Mental Training and Deep Coaching I was able to go back to my earliest memory of this 'feeling' and realised that as a four-year old boy caught up in the death of a deeply narcissistic and self-destructive family I was a victim of other people's misery.

When you realise that this distortion has been imposed on you and is not actually a part of yourself, you can let it go. The process of the resolution of this 'Dark Matter' is something like the process of tempering a Japanese sword blade.

By learning how to change the direction of my intention away from the 'Self of Now' the illusion dissolves and gives the Dark Matter nothing to act against. This is the QM4YS equivalent of 'Going Clear'.

Because of these distortions in our perceptions it makes it very difficult to repair ourselves alone.

We need someone to be a mirror to our deepest suffering and they need to be able to offer some kind of clarity at a time when we are consumed by the 'Self of Now'.

HOW TO BECOME UNBREAKABLE

Dark Matter is like a virus, once infected a person will tend to create even more Dark Matter and spread it to other living beings.

When you become caught up with Dark Matter and your life is turned upside down, you really only have two choices:

1. Let your pain destroy you and the people around you.

2. Learn to be 'unbreakable' by transforming the Dark Matter into light.

Pain is a little like a knocking coming from your car's engine. It's telling you what needs fixing in your life.

Take my body dysmorphia and self-hatred. Without that pain, I would never have known what needed fixing in my life! Because of that pain, I learnt to come to terms with childhood emotional and physical abuse.

The fundamental truth of all effective self-repair systems is that emotional and physical pain is there for a reason.

The best way to deal with our pain is to face it and not to fear it or try to avoid it.

That doesn't mean that we absolve those who have damaged us. That would have to be an entirely different conversation.

Neither does it mean that we learn to enjoy pain, these arguments are silly distractions from a profound truth.

The Holistic Universe conspires to help us wake up and evolve into exactly what we need to be. The events in our lives, no matter how difficult, are there for a reason.

With the help of a mixture of training, coaching and practice you too will overcome your challenges and become 'unbreakable'.

WHY SCIENTOLOGY MIGHT WORK BETTER THAN PSYCHIATRY

However you dress it up, Scientology works on the basis that some kind of negative energy seems to attach itself to the human psyche at various times in one's life, due to various forms of trauma. Most of the damage that is done to us happens when we are children.

The QM4YS system offers a rational explanation of why that is, indeed, the case.

Psychiatry, on the other hand, has no cures. Psychiatry is not designed to cure your suffering but to manage it.

When used on their own, systems like psychotherapy, Cognitive Behavioural Therapy and Neuro Linguistic Programming deal almost entirely with the person's symptoms rather than the underlying causes.

What is even more damaging is that these systems also focus entirely on the 'Self of Now', due to the fact that they admit only a mechanistic view of human life. These systems see human beings as 'lumbering robots' and therefore only really have half the story.

ARE SCIENTOLOGISTS THE ONLY ONES WITH A CURE?

The fundamental idea that 'Dark Matter' is created by the events of our lives is supported by Dr Peter Breggin's system of Empathic Therapy (although he would not use the term) (2).

Breggin's system is to identify 'Negative Legacy Emotions' and the events that triggered them. Once the emotion has been correctly identified, the patient is encouraged to restrict their reaction to that emotion. This is a process of mental training and self-discipline.

Once the patient has some success at restricting their Automatic Negative Thoughts, Breggin encourages the patient to 'Transcend' their trauma. (The word 'Transcend' is not explained.)

The concept of negative energy attaching itself to us at the moment of deep emotional damage is supported by many popular techniques of emotional and psychological repair. The problem for the Seeker is finding a way to see that damage clearly through the distortions in the Dark Crystal.

QUALITIES TO LOOK FOR IN A DEEP SPIRITUAL COACH

The Coach is there to be a mirror to the Seeker and should have the ability to separate themselves from their own 'Self of Now'. When we dissolve our own sense of 'self' we are able to truly empathise with the Seeker and serve them on the deepest level of truth.

The Coach must be truly present for the Seeker in a way that is more than your best friend ever could be. The Coach is not limited by a need to be liked or to please. The Deep Coaching process demands the highest level of honesty and courage from both the Seeker and the Coach.

It is the job of the Coach to be a reflection of the Seeker's 'Self of Tomorrow'.

It is vital to understand that the Coach is not there to 'fix' the Seeker. The only truth that matters is the truth of the Seeker. The process of Deep Coaching facilitates a holistic process of spiritual and emotional repair unique to the needs of the individual Seeker.

As we have demonstrated, the fundamental need of all living beings is deep connection at the level of the morphic field. In other words, we draw strength from each other. Together we are greater than the sum of our parts.

The problem that most of us face in trying to find a Deep Coach is that we only really trust our friends. Unfortunately, when it comes to our deepest problems most of us have a problem being honest with our friends.

Our own Dark Matter is a lot to lay on a friend and many friendships don't survive the process.

It should be possible to set up a network of Seekers local to you by putting an advert in the paper or on campus. This is the system that has worked for AA for so long.

Unfortunately, without the clarity and the support of Deep Coaching the path of repair can take a lifetime and condemn the Seeker to waste decades of life.

BECOME STRONGER AS A MENTOR

As you've seen with the above example from my own life, if we use guided meditation or some form of self-hypnosis (NLP or CBT) we may be able to affect some kind of temporary relief from the symptoms of our suffering but very quickly the old habits of thought reassert themselves.

This is the reason that in the QM4YS system we encourage those Seekers who have completed Academy Level One to volunteer for our 'Mentoring' programme. The best way for you to reinforce your own progress and ensure that the changes you make in your own life are permanent is to spend some time trying to help other people who are perhaps one step behind you.

We borrowed this idea from the Alcoholics Anonymous organisation. Its system of using 'Sponsors' is probably one of the main reasons that the AA has been so successful for the last 80 years.

To be honest, as someone who never really knew what a close family felt like, the mentoring programme is the part of QM4YS that I love the most. I don't think that I'm alone in the need for community and connection.

I hope that you will take strength from my obvious weakness because I know that 99% of the people who commit suicide do so because of a loss of connection to their own morphic field. It is my hope that together we can make that tragedy a thing of the past.

FLIGHT TO ABERDEEN

By the time I reached my gate, the flight was boarding. As the queue shuffled forward I was pushing my briefcase ahead of me, and trying to read a book on my iPad.

I was only ten metres or so from the gate when I heard some shouting and I noticed a security guard running toward us. Both of the kilted lads were roaring drunk. Obviously, last night's hangover had been turned into this morning's celebration.

My two friends from breakfast were arguing loudly with the ground crew. Security had wisely sent reinforcements and pulled them away from the gate.

As they were manhandled past me, the stench of stale sweat on nylon nearly made me lose my scrambled eggs and toast.

As I looked behind me, I noticed two men wearing Islamic prayer caps. They both smiled.

When we finally got on the plane, I located my seat by the window and soon found my Muslim friends were joining me in the same row.

I had spent most of my youth in the Middle East and have a great fondness for Arabia. We soon got talking about the differences in culture.

"When I see just how decadent Western culture has become, I often wonder what it is the British establishment expect Muslims to integrate into," said the Muslim gentleman next to me. He shook his head sadly.

"When my father arrived in London from Pakistan he was so proud to be in England! I'm glad he's not alive to see what it has become."

In a moment of clarity, I realised that there can never be healing and peace until we can see ourselves truly as we are.

Everyone in the UK is worried about Muslims but I suspect that we should be more concerned with the damage we do to our own culture.

I smiled and returned to my book.

****

THE QM4YS SYSTEM

As we dropped though the heavy Scottish clouds, Aberdeen lay like a granite fist on the emerald coast of the North Sea. Not so long ago I used to live here, in what was left of an ancient forest west of the city. That great forest had once covered this land like a lion's mane, from Hadrian's Wall to the Cairngorms.

I was lucky, I was first off the plane and, as I walked to the end of the Perspex exit tunnel, a taxi was already waiting for me.

As we silently rode into the city, I watched a landscape of grey houses and empty shops pass slowly by. Granite houses stood between fast food, mobile phone and betting shops like so many rotting teeth set in bloodless gums.

I realised that Scotland was dead on the inside; it has no love in it. My wife and I had left Scotland just as the nationalists had finally taken over.

Sadly Scottish nationalism is based more on a blind hatred for the English than it is on any love of the land. Hardly anybody speaks Gallic or Doric here, because (as they love to say) "they can't be arsed to learn." It wasn't always like this!

The Scots built the British Empire and, in all the ways that count, they are still a great people, but they've been conned into thinking of themselves as victims and bribed with the promise of unlimited free stuff. The Second World War drained Scotland of the best of its people.

Before the rise of this faux nationalism there was the Empire and before that there were the Clans. On the farm, where my house had been built, an ancient ring of stones still stood, like a memory of a different world.

A lot like American Indian Tribes, the Clan system had supported the Scottish people for thousands of years, but now everyone stands alone and lost.

Life doesn't have to be this way!

A DIFFERENT WAY OF SEEING

The Scottish Clans that lived near the standing stones of Clune, near my home, looked at the world in a very different way than do modern Scots.

Clan MacBeth and Clan Canmore were two of the larger clans in this area in the eleventh century and to them the Clan had a life of its own. According to Scottish folklore, every river, every tree and every standing stone had its own spirit or Sidhe.

In many ways, the Scottish Clans have more in common with the Lakota Sioux than the modern Scott.

For the Scottish Clans, the world around them was vitally alive but by the beginning of the first millennium, Christianity was in the process of dissolving the soul of the Scottish people and already the old ways were being forgotten but the Sidhe (fairies) were always there, just under the surface.

The taxi dropped me off at the client's offices. A faceless building in the middle of what had once been a forest. The door opened into a faceless foyer. The receptionist had mastered the art of passive aggression and assumed that I would be intimidated by her silence.

I ignored the visitor's book and the plastic badge she pushed toward me without looking up.

All I saw was a tired woman in a loveless world.

"Are you okay?" I asked with a worried smile.

"Er Yes! Well no! Not really! My car broke down and my bastard of a husband wouldn't drive me to work!" She blurted out. She looked surprised that she'd said so much.

"Well I'm glad you're here."

She looked so sad! It broke my heart. Life shouldn't be like this.

She frowned, considering my remark on its merits. Her sudden smile was like the sun coming out.

I sat down to wait and wondered what it would feel like to be a part of a Clan.

It occurred to me that you could take any child from any country in the world and if you throw them in the water they will all end up swimming in much the same way, in much the same style. Why is that?

How we swim is entirely determined by the reality of our bodies and the nature of the medium in which we swim.

At that moment in Scotland, I realised that the QM4YS system was a way for people to swim within the sub-atomic reality of the Holistic Universe and how we do that is determined by the nature of reality itself.

It follows then that the QM4YS system is not mine, it is in fact a part of all of us.

THE HOLISTIC WORLDVIEW

The Holistic Universe isn't something that you 'believe' in. Rather, it is something that you come to know through experience.

Through the process of making observations of the world around you and thinking deeply on some of the facts that I've brought to your attention, you will be able to open up your heart to the possibility of a different kind of life.

Because we are all so used to seeing Dr Feelgood statements on social media, we don't really stop to think about what it is that they're saying. It is vital for your well-being that you seriously consider the implications of the facts that I've presented for your review.

If we are all connected and if the world is set up exactly to support every moment of our lives, we can't go on living for the 'Self of Now'. We can't go on as we are, it makes no sense!

The fundamental core of the QM4YS system is the holistic worldview.

Many of life's problems dissolve away when we learn to look at the world from the perspective of the Holistic Universe.

That feeling of loneliness and separation melts away like the snow in the spring, when you realise that every living thing is a part of your family

You will come to see that the dreams, that once seemed impossible and beyond your grasp, are truly a future that is already a part of your life.

Like someone waking up from a coma, suddenly the world around you takes on a new beauty and significance. Rather than living in a dead and meaningless world, you will see that the world around you is alive and every moment of your life is of vital importance to all of us.

[Image 28: Symbol of the Holistic Universe.]

THE SACRED HOOP IS A SPIRAL

As I said, when we began this journey together, I'd been struggling to find a linear way to explain the Quantum Mechanics for Your Soul system. Unfortunately, life and the Holistic Universe just isn't like that!

It wasn't until Aberdeen that it hit me that 'real life' comes in spirals and not straight lines. There is only:

- *The illusion of the 'Self of Now'.*

- *Awareness and waking up to reality.*

- *The Matrix of the Holistic Universe.*

- *Repair of the Dark Matter — turning darkness into light.*

The QM4YS system IS the sacred hoop, because you can't gain control of the *'Self of Now'* unless you use the tools of *Awareness* in order to connect to the *Matrix* and you can't spiritually evolve unless you *Repair* the damage that has been done to your soul.

Each stage of your journey evolves into the next quite naturally in an eternal spiral of ascension but it all begins when we start to wake up to the 'Self of Now'.

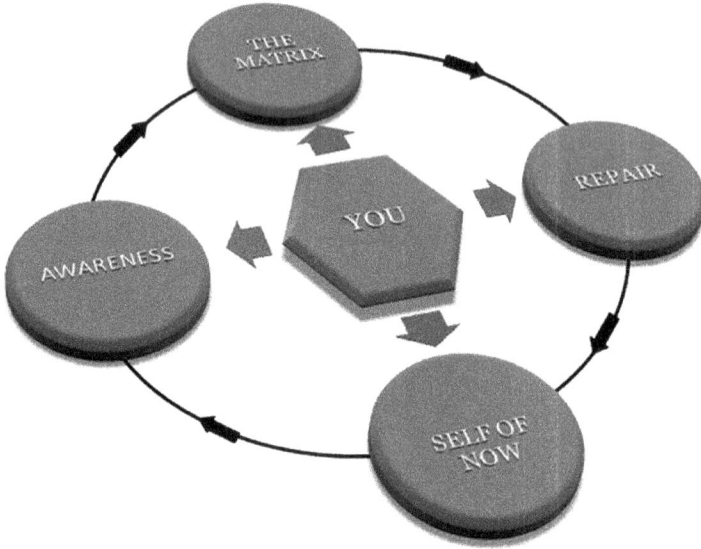

[Image 29: QM4YS Sacred Hoop.]

I. GETTING TO KNOW THE 'SELF OF NOW'.

The first step is for the Seeker to wake up to the 'Self of Now'.

Until we learn to notice the arising of the illusion of the 'Self of Now' no real progress can be made.

When we wake up to the fact that most of our life is lived on autopilot it gives us the determination to do something about our lives.

There are two aspects to the process of coming to know the 'Self of Now': external and internal.

External

The easiest way of noticing how the 'Self of Now' works is to see it in other people. You will begin to notice how people's actions are almost entirely automatic.

When we are able to be truly present in the moment, you will start to notice your own reactions to the situations you find yourself in and realise just how little of your real self goes into your life.

Internal

The next step is to try to notice the arising of the 'Self of Now' deep inside of you. Eventually you will notice the arising of the 'Self of Now' and learn how to become **Proactive** instead of **Reactive.**

The nature of the suffering that the 'Self of Now' presents to you is determined by the level of your awareness and the Dark Matter that exists in your life. It is for this reason that YOU are the only person who can fix you. It is vital, therefore, to learn to face yourself squarely and never flinch from the truth.

Ironically, the only way that we can find the clarity and the strength to do that is with the support of the people around us — our morphic field.

2. AWARENESS

Meditation, Mental Training or Inner Awareness is a problem because everyone thinks they know what it is.

As I said before, I used to work as Door Security so I know a little bit about violence. Do you remember the scene 'I know kung fu' in the film the Matrix? Pretty much any Hollywood action film these days will use some form of kung fu fight choreography.

Have you ever wondered why a real fight never looks anything like the fighting in a kung fu movie?

People shop for systems of fighting like children shop for sweets. We are attracted to the 'idea' of kung fu but we don't really like fighting. We like waving our arms around and believing that people can be killed cleanly with one touch but nobody likes getting hit! People shop for meditation in very much the same way. We want to feel all 'enlightened' and super transcendent. Maybe you like the austere beauty of Zazen or the spectacle of Sufi Dancing.

Maybe you like the utility of guided meditation for weekdays and save Vipissana for the weekend. When you approach meditation like this you are buying another 'idea' to add to your 'idea' of yourself.

You may hear different gurus chuntering on about how 'toning' is the new thing and how it will allow you to shift dimensions. This is like giving a monkey a typewriter, it's very amusing but can they write with it? Are they happier and more successful? Has 'toning' helped them fix themselves?

Altered states of consciousness have become the new 'thing', particularly in America. Worldwide there is a deep thirst for some kind of meaning in life and people are trying to tap into that. That's fine but here's the big 'But!' Look at the people who are trying to sell you the experience of a 'different' dimension or the 'ultimate' reality. Ask yourself this, 'Has their practice brought them anything but money'? Do you feel that they are spiritually evolved? Do you sense warmth and kindness from these people or a lust for cold hard cash?

If we approach 'meditation' looking for Transcendental Experiences or wanting to 'bend reality' then we will only ever be tourists within the Matrix. That doesn't mean that these teachers don't have valuable insights, it's just that they've settled for the waving of the arms and the legend of the 'death touch' instead of learning to fight. The danger of entering the Holistic Universe as a tourist is that you could get lost. You might even get mugged by the locals.

Kung fu is about fighting and meditation is about one thing only: changing the nature of your 'self'.

Meditation and indeed most spiritual practices become useless when we think of them as an end in themselves. In the QM4YS system we use most techniques of mental training but which system we use entirely depends on what the Seeker needs at this very moment.

In the QM4YS system, we understand that all living beings are forms of limitless energy that temporarily generate a physical body. The CPU of that body is the 'Self of Now'.

The underlying goal of your mental training therefore is only this: to change the direction of intention toward the Holistic Matrix.

It doesn't matter what religion you subscribe to, or what practice you use. Nor does it matter about your ability to 'jump dimensions' or use mirrors to astral project — who cares? Unless your daily practice changes you as a person and brings you closer to the Holistic Matrix nothing really matters.

That being said, apart from guided hypnosis, the QM4YS system uses most forms of meditation. We divide them into the following categories:

- *Concentration*
- *Reflection*
- *Sound*
- *Mantra*
- *Inner Journey*
- *Visualisation*

The multimedia course that accompanies this book includes a beginner's guide to mediation and a video demonstrating everything you would learn in a private one-to-one beginner's class. I will therefore not waste space here discussing the different techniques, as it would only fill your head with nonsense.

One final warning! Your 'Self of Now' will try to get you to use a meditation practice that will confirm his power over you. Magic boxes, secret knowledge and the promise of psychic powers will only inflate your ego and that has you travelling in exactly the wrong direction.

ESTABLISHING A PRACTICE

The most important part of your journey of self-repair is establishing a regular practice. It doesn't really take a great deal of time to begin, only ten minutes a day.

It is better to practice for five minutes with all your concentration rather than listen to a guided meditation for an hour and fall asleep.

We use techniques of sitting, standing and walking meditation.

If you can find the time to get out and connect to nature at least once a week, you will find it very helpful. But if you live in the city and can't get to the country, try to get somewhere high — rooftops are great but make sure you are safe.

3. CHANGING THE DIRECTION OF INTENTION TOWARD THE MATRIX

The QM4YS system is essentially the process of changing our direction of intention from centripetal contraction outward toward a centrifugal expansion.

Changing the Direction of Intention

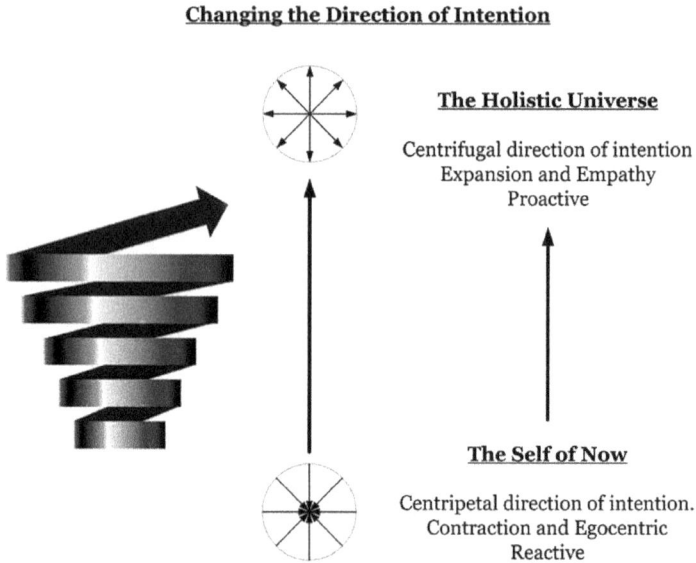

The Holistic Universe

Centrifugal direction of intention
Expansion and Empathy
Proactive

The Self of Now

Centripetal direction of intention.
Contraction and Egocentric
Reactive

[Image 30: Changing the direction of intention.]

The engine that drives the process of your self-repair is the continuing effort to change the direction of your intention from its initial focus on the 'Self of Now' and its inward contraction, out toward the Holistic Universe and a centrifugal expansion.

This is the 'gravity' that drives the process. Everything else is generated by, and is dependent on, your journey from the illusion of the 'Self of Now' toward the clarity of the 'Self of Tomorrow'.

Apparently, it really doesn't matter what ridiculous things you choose to believe, the only thing that matters is the direction of your intention and your determination to get more out of your life.

4. REPAIRING THE CRYSTAL AND DARK MATTER

Once we can restrict the darkness we make a little room for the light. When we can look within toward the 'Self of Tomorrow' we can see what we need to change in our self.

This is the other side of the Sacred Hoop where light begins to be controlled and contracted.

Through the process of work, we slowly restrict and correct our automatic reactions and cleanse the distortions in our Dark Crystal and try to deal with the Dark Matter that lay in wait for us out there in the world.

You will find that the natural gravity of your direction of intention will act like a Strange Attractor and pull you toward the changes you need to make in your life.

This is the point when a Deep Spiritual Coach becomes absolutely vital.

Most people find that as the 'Self of Now' dissolves, a sense of deep gratitude and joy emerges from the depth of our inner being.

Consciously, we make an effort to restrict our reactive nature whenever we can. Every time that you resist the urge to give in to your Automatic Negative Thoughts you will grow steadily stronger and stronger.

The goal at this point is to no longer live our lives as a reaction. We strive to be proactive instead of reactive.

The Seeker, with the aid of the Deep Spiritual Coach, will learn how to be totally present in the moment of their lives.

THE JOURNEY IS A SPIRAL

Including the foundation course, there are four levels in the QM4YS system. Each course is based on the same four foundational points but each level takes the student deeper within their own experience of themselves.

It can be helpful to think of the system as a spiral or a set of wheels within wheels.

The entire QM4YS system is designed to progressively unite the Seeker with the Holistic Universe or Matrix.

Have you ever looked at one of those children's puzzles where you have to see how many footballs are hidden in the jungle? You have to make your mind look at something familiar but in a different way.

I would like to say that, in order to repair yourself, you just have to follow a sequence of steps but in reality it is more like a puzzle or an illusion that resolves itself in your mind.

Everyone begins at the Foundation Level and after completing that you can enrol on the Academy Level One course, 'Fighting the Darkness'.

Each level is an evolving process of mental training and discipline. We work to identify the specific genesis of the suffering in life and use that knowledge as a guide to the repair of the Dark Crystal and the dissolution of the Dark Matter in our lives.

Note: Levels Two and Three are by invitation only.

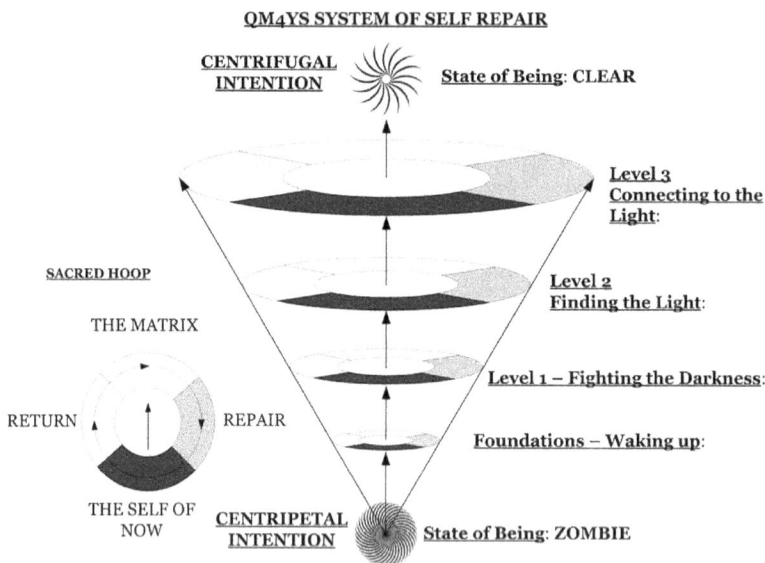

[Image 31: QM4YS System of Self-Repair.]

WORKING WITH ENERGY

Given the fact that we are beings of energy who temporarily generate physical bodies, it makes sense to try to keep that physical body healthy.

The physical body is generated from, and is controlled by, our energy body. It is vital to ensure that your energy body is as healthy as possible. The practice of Chi Gong (Energy Cultivation) gives us an opportunity to promote our health in a holistic and natural way.

A million years ago, I studied Oriental Medicine with Dr Lau in London but never got around to actually practicing medicine. I know from experience that in China, operations are regularly carried out without the use of general anaesthetic using only acupuncture. Recovery times are remarkably shorter when acupuncture is used to support healing.

The word 'Chi', in Mandarin, means Air + Rice. The energy in the body comes from oxygen and glucose so the word, 'Chi', makes a lot of sense from a scientific point of view (1).

Often we find that emotional and physical trauma is stored in, and expressed through, the body. The QM4YS system concentrates on trying to rebalance the harmony of the physical and energy bodies through the use of Chi Gong.

We harness the power of the breathing, concentration and physical movements to ensure the balanced flow of energy within the body.

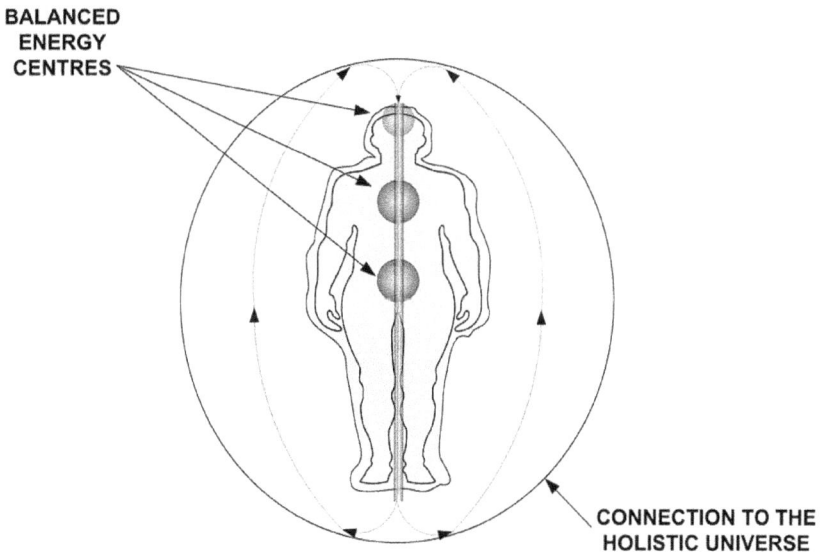

[Image 32: Shang, Zhong and Xia Dantians related to the Holistic Universe.]

Most gyms in the West have regular Tai Chi or traditional Yoga classes. If you are serious about trying to get more out of your life, you might like to consider taking some classes. Alternatively, check out our YouTube channel for free videos.

THE COMMUNITY

By far the biggest part of the QM4YS system is the importance of your connection to the world around you. Not everyone is lucky enough to be born into a big family or to have a lot of friends.

In order to provide a virtual and physical community of students, friends, mentors and tutors, we created the How Do I Fix Me Community. It is our intention that together we can change the world one person at a time.

Transcendental understandings are a total waste of time. In fact, they can be a source of fuel to the engine of the 'Self of Now' unless we bring those understandings into our everyday life.

The choice then is between evolving proactively or reactively. Unfortunately, if we wait to be prodded in the right direction, by the universe, life can get a little painful.

PROJECT DELAYED

My offshore project had been delayed due to the not inconsiderable problem of not having a boat. Our vessel would not be ready to be handed over to my client for another two days.

My briefcase was stuffed with drawings and notes for the project and I made my way down to the car park to wait for a taxi.

The magnetic door locked behind me with a click as I crunched across the gravel drive toward the main road.

It was midday but the wind cut me like a cheap French blade.

Beyond the ultramodern office building, the forest held what was left of last week's snow. I shivered.

"How could anyone live this far north?" I thought to myself.

A huge American style truck skidded to a halt and a mop of red hair appeared just above a grin as wide as a Cheshire cat's.

"You'll be needing a lift then?" He shouted.

Fergus was one of the best Subsea Inspection Engineers in the business and had been my second in command on many projects. I hadn't seen his name on the crew list.

"What the hell are you doing here?" I asked.

"Just off to buy a pony. You coming?"

Anything was better than standing in the grey cold of a Scottish spring. I climbed up into the cab and was surprised to find that it was almost as cold as the forest.

Fergus was wearing shorts and a t-shirt.

"Aren't you cold?"

"Aye! But it's nearly summer," he replied cheerfully as if that was an answer.

I decided to give up.

"Where're we going?" I said as I pulled my coat up around my neck.

"The standing stones near Tyrebagger."

"Near the airport," I said.

"Aye, I've promised Cati that I'd buy her a pony," Fergus said as he dropped the huge truck into second gear to scream past a cyclist.

The old man caught in the truck's slipstream wobbled like a Saturday night drunk on Union Street. Fergus looked in his wing mirror and laughed.

The stone circle on Tyrebagger Hill overlooks a farm imaginatively named, 'Standingstones' and it was to the farm that we were heading.

Aberdeenshire is full of standing stones and despite enthusiastically adopting a fundamentalist form of Calvinism many of the memories of the 'old' religion still exist.

We pulled into the farm and could see the stones glowing red in the afternoon sun; a memory of times long past. The stones are protected by a small wall on one side. The sun was already low and now touched the top of the trees that stood to one side of the stones.

The farmer came out to join us and noticed that we were both looking up at the stones.

"A lot of effort to make a calendar you'd think", he said as he came up to shake hands. He nodded toward the stones.

"You can use the stones to track the path of the Moon they say and I've found that the stones mess with the GPS on my drone."

"And there's me wanting to sacrifice virgins!" Fergus commented with a shrug.

The pony turned out to be not much bigger than my Rottweiler, which was just as well. Fergus was often mistaken for one of the Dwarves in Lord of the Rings. The men of the north had ridden ponies like this to war.

More used to Spanish horses, I tried to hide my contempt.

"She won't have far to fall," I offered helpfully.

Fergus eyed me suspiciously as he was well used to my sarcasm. He decided to change the subject.

"You'll have to see the wee church we're renovating. How's that pile you're working on in Spain?"

My wife and I had been trying to renovate an old farm in Spain with not much success.

He sniffed and told the farmer that he needed a bigger pony.

"C'mon man, I've left Mary painting. You'll stay for a spot of tea?"

We left the dejected pony with its owner and climbed into Fergus' truck.

CHAPTER 13

****

HOW TO SAVE YOURSELF

My farm in the mountains of northern Spain lay on the road to Santiago de Compostela (Saint James of the Field of Stars) not far from the walled city of Morella. We had spent a small fortune trying to reintroduce the Granacha grape and revive what had once been a successful vineyard before the Civil War.

I had made the mistake of buying the farm, as a half renovated project, from an Englishman. The main house had swallowed up some barns in the 1800s and sprawled down a slope toward the mountainside and a series of terraces cut a thousand years ago by Christian slaves for their new Arab masters.

Dodgy Desmond had dropped the level of half the house but failed to account for the power of the autumn storms in the mountains of Castellon. We spent most of September watching our Indian furniture float past us toward the lower barn doors.

The problem with any repair of an old house is the urge to paint what should be rebuilt.

Dodgy Desmond had bought and renovated several properties on our mountain and left the countryside strewn with overly optimistic buyers trying to 'crowd fund' his assassination.

Desmond professed to be a master of Reiki and the victim of his wife's demise. As it turned out, he was a divorced, part-time car salesman and full-time confidence trickster from Nuneaton.

He'd used carved angels as a way to deflect attention from the failing plumbing and the leaking cesspit. I'm ashamed to say that it had worked, in spades!

He had so reminded me of my half-Jewish father that I'd fallen for the old fraud, hook, line and sinker.

"Well? Whatdoyathink?" Fergus said from the right side of his face, jolting me back to reality.

Despite growing up in London, I still needed a translator in Scotland. I had once spent an entire morning joining every queue in the Heliport because I couldn't understand a word the tannoy said.

Fergus and his wife had bought an old church and were in the middle of turning it into a home.

The 'Wee Church' was a form of Protestant Christianity unique to Scotland. The Scottish Church had been an enthusiastic supporter of the Frenchman Jean Calvin in his rebellion against Rome and its Pope. In the mid 1800s the Scottish Church had split once again and its people had dutifully given their hard earned cash to their newly independent form of Christianity.

For a hundred years, they had generously built so many churches that by the time of the Second World War a German soldier could have parachuted into Scotland and thrown a stone in any direction and he would have been guaranteed to hit a church.

For the last fifty years, the 'Wee Church' had been selling off those churches like a sinking ship loses passengers, most of which had been turned into strip clubs and bars for the new lords of the oil business.

The church that Fergus and his wife had just adopted stood on a cliff and overlooked the North Sea.

"You do know that all those beams have woodworm?" I reluctantly pointed out.

Fergus looked at Mary for support. She made a face that said, 'you're on your own'.

"What makes you think they've got woodworm?" He said defensively.

"The holes, the dust on the floor and the way the beams are sagging."

"I thought that was just the age!"

PAINTING OVER WOODWORM

Trying to repair your life is a lot like trying to renovate an old house. It's hard to even know where to start. Often we ask ourselves, is it even possible?

What we create in life is really a product of what we believe. Until May 1954 the world believed that nobody could run a mile in less than four minutes. After Roger Banister did it, it has become relatively common. The world didn't believe it possible to run a sub-four minute mile so nobody did!

This is why it is so important to question our worldview, our assumptions and prejudices. If Fergus and his wife didn't have a deep love for that old church, how it fits into the landscape, and the lives of the people around it, maybe they would have just let the building fall into the sea or turn it into another McDonald's.

The materialistic worldview is like a cataract that has made us blind to the world around us. Just like the gorilla demonstrated in the basketball game, people see what they expect to see.

People assume that their lives are meaningless and that they are alone. Because of this assumption, they get depressed and eventually kill themselves.

We have been robbed of our belief in our own ability to understand the world around us. It is this assumption that keeps us slaves of a corrosive system.

That our system is corrosive cannot be denied.

I know that some people will find it very uncomfortable to question their belief in materialism and all the dogma that it implies. It will also be tempting for some people to get caught up arguing over some of the individual points that I've made.

We could argue endlessly about red-shifts, warped space and gravitons but I would suggest that you look at the preponderance of the evidence that I've presented, rather than fixate on winning an intellectual war. I would argue that putting these cutting edge scientific hypothesis together lends them a weight greater than the sum of their parts.

By all means, you can choose to believe whatever you like. If you insist on believing that your life is entirely accidental and therefore, inherently without meaning that is entirely your right and I wish you joy of it.

Unfortunately, your presuppositions mean that there is nothing I can do to help you. Indeed, you are as alone as you believe you are.

Similarly, if you try to renovate a building and only see bricks and dollars, you will only ever create something empty and meaningless.

It is also entirely pointless putting new paint over beams rotten with woodworm. New Age gobbledygook based on wishes rather than reality is also entirely pointless.

It is for this reason that a holistic understanding of the sub-atomic world is so important. It gives us a solid base from which to begin.

I want you to take a deep breath and look at yourself in the mirror. Realise this, 'In all the universe, you are unique and so is every other living being. Your life is connected to every atom in the universe and you are not alone. Your life is as precious to me as my own'.

Now! If you approach the task of sorting out your life with this as your 'backstory' I guarantee that together we will create a work of art.

SO WHERE DO YOU BEGIN

Fergus' renovation of the church in Scotland would never work if he didn't first get an accurate picture of exactly what was wrong with it.

He had seen the holes in the beam, the way that it sagged and the dust on the floor, those are facts. Like our feelings of discontent, despair and our suffering in life are a fact.

Both Fergus and I, when we bought our ancient farms, had been blind to their underlying problems simply because our desire predisposed us to ignore them.

Neither did we have an overall understanding of the mechanisms by which an old house deteriorates.

This is the problem you now face regarding your own life. You need to get a clear picture of exactly what is going on inside of you and where you are in the world. Take the time to examine the dependent origination of all that's in your life.

Now that you understand the mechanisms of Dark Matter you can look at your life and see what needs to be repaired.

With that in mind, take some time to make a quiet assessment of your life and how you feel about it. Think about where you are and where you want to be in five years. Look for repeating patterns of suffering and stress.

To help you achieve this initial assessment, the QM4YS system has prepared a series of free tools that will help you focus and gain some clarity. You can download them free from our website.

- *A complete multimedia step-by-step guide to meditation.*

- *A 28 Day multimedia foundation course with a detailed workbook to help you begin a system of introspection.*

- *AWARENESS:* A series of specific worksheets focused on helping you to become aware of your underlying issues and inner life.

- *CONTROL:* A series of specific worksheets to help you learn to master the 'Self of Now'.

- *REPAIR:* A series of specific worksheets to help you begin the repair and renovation process.

- *Facebook Group:* You can connect to our community and ask questions in our closed group.

- *Forum:* If you would like more privacy you can join our forum on the website to ask questions of current students and of the How Do I Fix Me community.

FIRST STEPS

As you begin your journey toward self-repair it is vital that you keep several things in mind:

- Realise that you are not your thoughts and emotions. They are just like woodworm in Fergus' beams, they are just symptoms of the 'Self of Now'. Refuse to identify with your suffering.

- Remember that you are not alone. Your success is vital to all of us. Don't be ashamed to reach out for help and support.

- Take responsibility for your life. That doesn't mean that if you were abused it was your fault. If you were unfortunately abused there's nothing in this world that can un-abuse you. You can't change the past but you can change your future.

- Take responsibility for your reaction to what has happened in your life. If you hang onto the damage that people have caused you then it will always define you and it will pull you down like a stone. Become unbreakable. Refuse to pass on the Dark Matter that has already infected your life.

- Trust that the Matrix will help you. Learn to truly listen inside and you will know just what to do for the best.

- Make space and time to be quiet. Begin a daily practice of mental training and start keeping a personal journal. The foundation course workbook is a good start here.

- Make sure, if you can, that you get plenty of good quality sleep.

- Try to get outside at least once a day, have a walk and get some fresh air.

- Try to cut down on artificial stimulants. You are trying to get a clear picture of what is going on inside of yourself so clarity is the keyword here.

DEALING WITH THE DARKNESS

The sad truth of life is that every time we focus our intention through the prism of the 'Self of Now' (Dark Crystal) we can't help but create suffering.

In the past we have all created suffering and other people have damaged us in return.

The goal is to deal with Dark Matter within ourselves and the world around us.

For example, when I was a boy my mother and I were desperately poor. My mother used to get up and light our one coal fire. I can still hear her shovelling coal in the snow and chopping kindling.

She had a perfectly healthy son in me but I can't remember ever trying to take that chore from my poor aging mother. Every time I think of my mother, I want to die with shame. She deserved a better son than me!

There is nothing that I can do about that now but what I can do is get up and light the fires and put on the coffee for my own family and every day, I think of my mother and honour her memory and beg her forgiveness.

In this way, through action, we can work toward turning 'Dark Matter' into light.

In order to overcome our negative legacy emotions (depression, anxiety, anger, shame), we have to deal with the 'darkness' that was created by other people as well as ourselves.

Like Jeffrey Dahmer, often it is our own reactions to that damage that causes yet more 'Darkness'.

Using mental training (meditation) and self-repair, we work to identify our Negative Legacy Emotions, take control of our reactions to them and eventually transcend those feelings by connecting to the Holistic Matrix.

Depression, anger, shame, and anxiety are reflections of the damage within. They are reactions that point to what you need to change in your life. Human suffering is designed to push us toward the repair of ourselves.

PURPOSE IN LIFE

None of us are here by accident. Every one of us is vital to everyone else. We, each of us, have a purpose to fulfil. We have skills and gifts that are for us alone to share.

When you learn to embrace life as a living thing, and each day as your last, suddenly all of the things that were stopping you realise your potential fall away. When you stop feeding the Black Wolf you will find that you are free to truly be yourself.

All mistakes are a way that the universe teaches us but the only crime you can commit in this life is to die without truly having found your purpose.

Remember, it is not what you achieve that makes a great life; it's what you overcome. It may be that your true purpose was to overcome impossible odds.

As you erode the 'Self of Now' you will find the 'Self of Tomorrow' will emerge like a butterfly from its chrysalis. You will find a purpose in life that will set fire to your soul.

A MOVIE OF YOUR LIFE

Another important point to remember is that your life is a movie. Whatever appears in your movie is there for a very good reason. Everything is a clue.

Like most Hollywood stories, most people come to 'self-repair' because of an event in their lives.

Most people give up when they forget about the reason that they began. That's a shame. That's like waking up from a coma, going out for dinner and then asking the doctor to put you back to sleep.

It is the purpose of your life to choose what goes into your movie. You can't tell the story of how you got to play cello in the Sydney Opera House without telling us how you overcame incredible hardship to learn to play the cello.

The movie of your life must have a backstory and some effort. Embrace the difficulties and the challenges; face them head on because you can decide how the story ends if you want to.

Finding out what your purpose is in life comes as a by-product of getting to know the real you.

SOWING SEEDS

The 'Self of Now' will try to convince you that you need this person or that thing. Maybe you long for the girl or guy you couldn't have when you were young.

You might watch a hero in a film make love to his woman and look at your husband and think 'if only'! We are even encouraged to think this way by the media but it is incredibly corrosive and inherently wrong! Why?

Because we are sowing seeds that will result in nothing but tears. We are sowing the seeds of 'Dark Matter'.

When we look at the things in our life as the fruit of the entire universe, which has produced these things just for us, we begin to see just how rich we really are. When we look at life in this way we are sowing seeds in our lives that will bear fruit for the rest of our lives and beyond.

BE PROACTIVE, NOT REACTIVE

I grew up in London and in that world you were judged by your capacity for violence.

Contrary to what you would expect, the one thing I learnt was the ability to NOT react. In a world of violence, control is the essence of power.

Weakness means that you are a slave to your reactions. Power means that you can control you. When you can control yourself, you can control others.

When someone says something you don't like, pause. Breathe out. Let it go. You will know in your heart what you need to say.

Download and use our proactivity worksheets to help you with this.

To help us understand just how to apply the QM4YS system in your own life, let's examine three recent case studies. We've changed the names of the individuals involved to protect their privacy but the details of the case studies are a true account of their process of repair.

CASE STUDY #1

Name: Mark W.

Sex: Male

Age: 34 years

When Mark first joined our community, he had just suffered a breakdown and had been diagnosed as Bi-Polar and had a history of addictive sexual habits. Use of drugs had caused a severe disassociation with reality.

After completing the foundation course, and establishing a daily meditation practice, Mark was able to realise for himself that his depression was just a product of the 'Self of Now'. He was able to reduce his compulsive behaviour but still struggled with feelings of anxiety.

During Deep Coaching, we established that Mark's inappropriate sexual compulsion was a coping mechanism that sought to deal with the underlying feelings of anxiety and rejection. Eventually Mark was able to realise that his feelings of anxiety and rejection began when he was a six-year-old boy as a response to the situation he found himself in.

By learning to trust the Holistic Matrix, Mark was able to let go of his anxiety. Using our Emergency S.T.O.P.P worksheet, Mark was able to take control of his compulsions.

Mark set himself the goal of learning to teach English as a foreign language and travel to foreign counties.

CASE STUDY #2

Name: Emily B.

Sex: Female

Age: 25 years

When Emily joined our community, she had suffered from sexual abuse when she was eight-years-old by her mother's boyfriend. She was rejected by her father and family.

She moved to London when she was 16 years old and had managed to work her way through university on her own.

She was suffering from chronic anxiety and was also diagnosed with depression. She also reported having a drink problem that she wanted to overcome.

After completing the foundation course, Emily was able bring her drinking under some kind of control. She began a series of Deep Coaching sessions in which she confessed to a revulsion of her own sexuality.

After a few weeks, Emily had a breakthrough and realised that her self-loathing came from the rejection she suffered by her father and his family. Subconsciously she had taken the rejection as confirmation that the abuse she suffered was her fault.

We were able to use some re-framing and some grounding techniques to help Emily overcome her anxiety in the short-term. Using daily meditation training Emily was able to let her pain go and move on with her life.

She set herself the goal of forming a strong long-term relationship, which she did.

CASE STUDY #3

Name: Katherine S.

Sex: Female

Age: 45 years

Katherine had been in an abusive relationship and was single at the time of joining the community. However, she was only really looking to find some way to get more out of her life. She had not previously visited a mental health professional.

She said, she just felt that life was so empty.

Katherine completed the foundation course and had a series of Deep Coaching sessions over two months.

By the end of her training, Katherine reported that she now enjoyed every day of her life. She had learned to see every problem in life as an opportunity. She had become aware of the arising of her thoughts and had learned to restrict the arising of the 'Self of Now'.

Recently, Katherine contacted us to share an update; she had come to terms with the fact that she had been passive aggressive with her first husband and had instigated many of their problems. She had recently formed a new relationship and had been able to learn to let go of her own aggression in order to form a direct and trusting connection.

CLIMBING THE MOUNTAIN FOR YOURSELF

Remember to never mistake the map for the terrain! What do I mean?

Let me tell you a story:

There is a mountain behind our village. Many years ago, I decided to climb it. I trained for two years to prepare for my journey. I learnt to use ropes and to climb a sheer cliff. It nearly cost me my life but I eventually managed to climb that mountain and stand at the top.

I could tell you the story of my adventure. You could take detailed notes and create a map. You could make illustrations from my descriptions and publish a book. This book would make you rich.

You could tell people that you climbed the mountain yourself. Maybe you would be invited by famous journalists to be interviewed on TV. It would be great.

But afterwards, lying alone and awake in the hotel room, you would still be the same old you. The book about the mountain would not have changed anything in your life. The moment you told the lie, the moment you took my experience for your own, a wall was built in your soul between you and that mountain.

All religions, all beliefs are like that book: the shadow of someone else's life. The moment we take their story for our own we build a wall between us and reality.

We make it effectively impossible for ourselves to change and grow.

The 'QM4YS' system is a guide book, a Haynes workshop manual! On its own it is useless. You have to do the work yourself.

You have to make the journey up that mountain for yourself. That mountain is your birthright.

If I had known, when I was young, what I now know, I could have saved myself an awful lot of suffering. The emotional and physical abuse that I suffered as a boy would not have maimed my life as it did. The emotional problems that drove me to travel the world would have dissolved away like morning mist.

For those of you who are determined to get more out of life and to take your journey to the next level, we do provide several courses that form a basis for our tailor-made one-to-one coaching.

On Level One of the Mechanics for your Soul system - Fighting the Darkness, you will have an hour and ten minutes one-to-one tuition to spread out over the time of your course. (Usually eight weeks).

THE ACADEMY IS THE ULTIMATE 'RED PILL'.

There are four courses in the Academy: Foundation, Levels One, Two and Three. Each course takes you progressively deeper down the 'Rabbit Hole'.

The suffering of modern life is caused by our illusions. We see the world through the crystal of the self and fail to see life as it really is. We live in a world we create with our mind.

The Academy courses are designed to help you examine your preconceptions and illusions in a fun and engaging way. Through the support of the community, we bring your new clarity, and its implications, into your daily life.

WHO ARE THE ACADEMY COURSES FOR?:
- *Struggling to connect to the people around you*
- *Lack self-confidence*
- *Want to get 'more' out of life and find your true purpose*
- *If you are struggling with depression*

- *Feeling anxious and nervous*
- *Feel disconnected and remote from life*
- *Living with grief*
- *Anger management issues*
- *Fighting addictions*

ACADEMY COURSES: WHAT YOU GET:

- *Courses are tailored to suit individual students*
- *Weekly ONE-TO-ONE contact with your Tutor via Skype, Zoom, WhatsApp, or email*
- *Assigned a Mentor from within the Community*
- *Modular courses that progressively repair the soul*
- *Designed to directly reconnect the 'self' to the moment*
- *Based on science, observable fact and not religion*
- *Multimedia course materials are electronic download for you to keep. Physical course materials are available at extra cost*
- *The opportunity to Mentor new students*
- *Become a part of a vibrant worldwide community*

QM4YS - ACADEMY LEVEL ONE:

Academy Level One builds on your successes in the foundation course. It is designed to be completed over eight weeks but it is up to you if you would like to take longer.

The heart of the course is your contact with the community. The course fee includes an initial orientation meeting with your tutor via Skype, Zoom, WhatsApp or Google Hangout.

You also get an hour one-to-one coaching spread over the time of your course.

All of the multimedia materials are available for download and can be studied in your own time. You will not need a constant internet connection to complete the course.

WHAT YOU GET WITH THE LEVEL ONE COURSE:

- *Course Manual*

- *Meditation Course Level 2*

- *Course Workbook*

- *Questionnaires*

- *Eight Video Lectures*

- *One-to-One Tuition 60 min plus 10 min orientation interview*

- *Course Mentor*

- *Private Online Support Forum and Facebook Group*

- *Eight Week Course*

ACADEMY LEVEL ONE – FIGHTING THE DARKNESS – EXAMINES:

- *Finding the Matrix Within:* Learn to detach from the arising of the 'Self of Now' and experience a connection to the Holistic Universe. Multimedia meditation course that builds on the training in the foundation course.

- *Belief Vs. Knowing:* We examine what we believe and why. How belief is communicated through the use of story and image. Learn to see how the self is born from the sum of our past, what we 'believe' about that past and our expectations for the future. Building on the introduction to this subject in the 28 Day Foundation Course, we learn to watch the arising of belief.

- *The Electromagnetic Universe:* Through the use of experiments and exercises we explore the implications of the EM Rope hypothesis and morphic resonance on the sub-atomic universe. For those who are interested, there is an opportunity to explore the science behind the QM4YS system in more detail.

- *Dealing with the Dark Crystal:* Children are born innocent! The damage that is done to us when we are children, before we can defend ourselves, burns holes in our souls that distort how we look at the world for the rest of our lives. Symptoms of this damage are founded in guilt, shame and anxiety. Identify and begin the repair of your Dark Crystal.

- **What is 'Lasting Fulfilment':** Materialism teaches us that happiness is a reaction. This section of the course examines what it takes to provide us with long-term fulfilment and contentment as opposed to short-term happiness and pleasure.

- **Restricting the 'Self of Now':** Learn how to recognise the arising of the 'Self of Now' and feel the solidification of your worst enemy: yourself. Explore the implication of our self-destructive nature in our everyday life.

- **Being the 'Cause' and not the 'Effect':** We live our lives like dogs chasing cars. We live our lives almost entirely reactively. Our 'happiness' is almost totally the product of the accidents in our life. This part of the course helps you begin to be the cause instead of the effect.

- **Seeing life as a continuum rather than a polaroid:** So many times in life we don't realise what we have until it's too late. In this part of the course we learn how to change how we look at life and how to embrace the changes.

- **Fighting the Darkness:** Negativity is a bit like sliding down the helter skelter in the fair; we spin around and around but always we go down. This section of the course looks at how we tend to magnify the darkness in our lives without meaning to. We look at the tools you can use to rebalance your life and reduce the amount of suffering you experience. We look at how we can protect ourselves from negativity, both our own and other people's.

Academy Levels 2 and 3 are by invitation only.

SPIRITUAL PRACTICES IN A MODERN WORLD

For most of my life, I've taught martial arts. In most martial arts we have sets of ritualised movements called 'forms' or 'Kata'. These sets of movements are sometimes hundreds of years old.

If you practice a set of slow movements with fixed attention and visualisation of the movement's application, when you come to actual combat you will find that you have programmed your automatic reflexes to move in a certain way. Without that clear intention the movements are just an empty dance.

Today, people often perform these movements but they don't really know what the movement is for. Unfortunately, without the fixed intention the movements are useless.

Spiritual practices are something like this. What was once the spontaneous expression of someone's inner life, religious spiritual practices and rituals often end up just being indications of tribal identity.

It can be a lot of fun getting dressed up and mincing around in a 'look at me' outfit but you are just feeding the 'Self of Now'. From the point of view of true spiritual and emotional evolution, it is better to keep your spiritual practices intensely private. In this way you can avoid feeding the 'Self of Now'.

There are, however, a few principles that seem to be reoccurring themes throughout the history of humanity. Within the context of the QM4YS system, we have learnt how Dark Matter seems to have a contagious affect on the world around us and appears to be transmitted from one person to another. For this reason, you might find it interesting to consider the following:

WATER

Pure water is diamagnetic and a poor electrical conductor. That means that it shouldn't be affected by magnetic fields, neither should it conduct electricity. Despite those two physical facts, water manages to do both quite well.

Water is attracted to both positive and negative charge and its ability to absorb means that the salts within ordinary water makes it a great conductor of electricity. Throughout history, water has been used to cleanse objects, places and people from the contamination of negative energy.

For this reason, you might find it helpful to make it a habit to always wash your feet, hands and face before your daily meditation practice.

Making sure that your living space is kept as clean as possible also helps to avoid negative contamination. If you've spent time with very negative people and you feel drained, it is a good idea to take a deep bath, if you have that facility.

INCENSE

It's a good idea to burn incense during your practice, as your sense of smell is hard-wired to your subconscious mind. When you create an altered state of consciousness in practice, when you smell the same scent in the future your mind will readily recreate the same state of mind. In a way you can use incense to encourage a Pavlovian response in your own mind.

BOWING

There is a reason that most cultures throughout human history have used the practice of bowing in their day-to-day religious practice, it's a great way to shrink the 'Self of Now'. If it is something that resonates with you, try bowing before and after your practice sessions and see how it makes you feel.

Just make sure that you keep your training sessions private because the moment that we try to make our practice an excuse to show-off, we end up inflating the 'Self of Now' and this will be counter-productive to your goals.

Remember! Only you can say what is right for you. Most of us end up with similar habits but it would be a huge mistake to share them at this point. When it is time for you to express your inner reality externally you will know, because you won't have any other choice.

The QM4YS is designed to facilitate the evolution of your consciousness and thereby affect the change of the entire world. Just as one tuning fork communicates a note to another, transcendental reality resolves itself quite naturally within you and harmoniously communicates to you the rhythm of life.

THE DYING LAND

In 1244, Alexander II then King of Scotland gifted one thousand acres of land southwest of Aberdeen to the Church. In the sixteenth century, a bishop took it for himself. Today that land belongs to an international chain of hotels.

As the car swung into the drive leading up to my hotel, I wondered what it would have been like to call this Victorian mansion 'home'.

Fergus' monster truck scattered the gravel drive as we skidded to a halt beside the carved lions of the grand entrance. A few years ago, a doorman used to come out and help you with your bags but these days everyone is on their own.

Ardoe House was built by a soap merchant on land stolen from the people by the church. Luckily for me it was turned into a hotel in 1947.

My room had a view out over the land heading south. I used to live nearby, before the price of oil crashed. We used to have a well but the water was poisoned by the farmers, you couldn't drink it! The pesticides and chemicals from the land had poisoned the water table.

As the idea of the 'clan' has died, the people have become divorced from the land. Toward the river I could see fields of cattle grazing, or what now passes for cattle. They are usually full of steroids and antibiotics and live half the time they did when I was a boy.

How did we get to this desolate place so quickly? The dying land is a symptom of the desolation within each one of us. Until we heal ourselves how can we even think of healing the planet?

CHAPTER 14

****

HOW TO SAVE THE WORLD

Watching the sun set behind the river I try to imagine this Subarctic landscape back in the day when Macbeth was the Lord here.

Shakespeare's version of the story has a man of honour sell his soul to satisfy his wife's ambitions and, in the process, destroys everything he loves including his wife and children.

In the evening sun, a herd of cattle wander toward the gate of their enclosure as the farmer tips buckets of food on the ground.

Their bodies were not designed to eat the food that he's giving them. Corn fattens them quicker than grass but irreparably damages their bodies at the same time. To overcome this problem, they are given vitamins and antibiotics to prolong their lives long enough for the farmer to profit from their death.

I am reminded of prisoners in WW2 death camp. The cattle have the same look of resignation in their eyes. How quickly humanity has set about the destruction of everything that made human life worth living.

A hundred years of materialism has created a perfect existential storm.

OUR BRAVE NEW WORLD

The 'establishment' promotes the idea that human life is a virus on the face of the Earth. They like to scare the shit out of everyone and then insist that some existential threat can only be addressed by their use of taxation. This stratagem has served them well for the last fifty years. It diverts attention away from the banks, their companies, and the irreparable damage that they themselves are doing to the planet.

The evil that is consuming our planet could only exist within the corrosive worldview that the establishment and the elites have created. Despite half a century of political and social activism things are getting worse, fast. Why?

War is chaos and if you find yourself within the confusion of the battle facing in the same direction as your enemies, it is usually safe to assume that you are lost and are facing the wrong way.

If you find yourself with a sign in your hand protesting for something that the government already support, you may like to consider the fact that you are more a part of the problem than the solution. Don't bother signalling your virtue because you are working for the enemy.

As with self-repair, there are no easy answers when it comes to saving the planet. To understand the radical answer, you need to understand the incredible profundity of the problem.

FACTORY FARMING:

In the 1920s some sociopath of a scientist came up with the idea of keeping farm animals in giant warehouses. He found that animals didn't need sunlight if you give them enough vitamin A and D (1).

A farmer can maximise his profits by cramming as many animals as possible into the smallest space. Unfortunately, this increases the spread of disease. To counter this threat, farmers regularly give the animals antibiotics. In fact over 80% of world antibiotic production is given to animals in factory farms. Predictably enough, the United States leads the way when it comes to factory farming.

Chickens have their beaks and claws cut off to stop them killing each other. They are fed so many steroids that they grow too quickly and to such massive sizes that they can't support their own weight. Male chicks serve no purpose to the egg business so they are ground up on day one (2).

Newborn calves are taken from their mothers at birth and are not allowed to drink her milk, which is for human consumption only. Cows are regularly injected with antibiotics and steroids (3).

Pigs live in small concrete boxes full of their own manure and because of that 65% of Pigs have pneumonia. Pregnant sows are kept in cages so they can't turn around (4).

All farm animals are fed GMO foods, which their bodies were not designed to digest. GMO foods would eventually kill them if they lived long enough. Seventy-five years ago a cow on a farm would live for 4-5 years. Today she is lucky to see her second birthday.

Obviously, mass medication in large populations is inherently dangerous and encourages the growth of 'super-bugs'. I'm just waiting for the zombie apocalypse (5).

As farmers push to maximise their profits, more and more inhumane practices are adopted with no thought for animal welfare. With the increase in animal suffering, any meat produced is inevitably compromised by the chemicals that all living things secrete under stress conditions. But as it's not the farmer that is going to eat the product, they really don't care!

The horrors and cruelty that are visited on animals in the name of factory farming are exceeded only by the torture inflicted on them in the name of science.

There is no test too unthinkable for a scientist not to think of it (6).

And if you're thinking that you are not a part of the problem because you are a vegan, think again!

John Francis Queeny was a member of the Catholic organisation, The Knights of Malta. He was married to Olga Mendez Monsanto. In 1901, he started the now infamous company called Monsanto (7).

Monsanto's first product was an artificial sweetener called, 'saccharin', which they supplied to Coca-Cola. The American government knew that saccharin was poisonous and sued to stop its manufacture but lost the case in court.

Queeny's company never looked back. Nobody, including the American Government, could stop Monsanto.

In order to produce enough vegetarian food for people, entire ecosystems must be destroyed and given over to industrial agriculture. This kind of farming destroys topsoil, so production can only be maintained by using chemical nitrates.

Most of the chemicals used in industrial agriculture are manufactured by Monsanto.

Half of the Earth's topsoil has been lost in the last 150 years (8).

It takes 300 years to replace one inch of topsoil.

Scientific American quoted Reuters,

"Only 60 Years of Farming Left if Soil Degradation Continues."

Forget 'Global Warming', without topsoil we will all starve to death!

CHEMICAL CASTRATION? JUST EAT SOY

Ninety-three percent of world Soy production is genetically modified to resist Monsanto pesticides. Why would they do such a thing? Money! Unfortunately, soy might not be vulnerable to pesticides but you are (9)!

Any kind of GM Soy is full of hormones and can cause problems with your health.

Soy contains: Phytoestrogens, Goitrogens, Phytates and Trypsin.

- *Phytoestrogens* – are plant derived estrogens that imitate estrogen and therefore effectively raise the estrogen lowering testosterone level (hence chemical castration for 'Soy Boys').

- *Goitrogens* – actively suppress thyroid function. They actually restrict the thyroid from getting the right amount of iodine from the diet.

- *Phytates* – are enzyme inhibitors that block mineral absorption in the human digestive tract.

- *Trypsin* – is a digestive enzyme that we need to properly digest protein. Soy is rich in trypsin inhibitors.

Thousands of studies link unfermented soy to malnutrition, digestive distress, immune-system breakdown, cognitive decline, reproductive disorders, cancer and heart disease.

Soy crops are probably the most destructive of all the mono-crops, as it takes all of the nutrition from the land and puts nothing back.

FRANKENSTEIN CROPS

As a young man in the 1980s I fought for Greenpeace and the Green Party against the spread of Genetically Modified Crops but we were wasting our time. Monsanto owns the patents on GMO Corn and Wheat so it was case closed.

GMO was released into the UK by 'accident' so the government shrugged its shoulders and let Monsanto get on with what it does best.

There are thousands of reports out there that explain the dangers of GMO Wheat and Corn so I won't bore you here. You can find more details on our website if you are interested (10).

THE DEADLY SUGAR FREE OPTIONS

Our friends at Monsanto, with the help of Donald Rumsfeld (who served George W. Bush as Secretary of Defence), modified the E-Coli bacteria to defecate aspartame (11).

The chemical is in nearly all processed foods. I know from personal experience that long-term use of this chemical damages the digestive tract. If stored at temperatures above 29.4 degrees centigrade, the aspartame breaks down in to neurotoxic substances that have been linked to the Gulf War Syndrome.

PLASTIC POISON

Over 17 million barrels of oil are required just to produce the plastics that make bottled water. That is more than the entire aviation sector. At least eight million tons of plastics are dumped into the oceans every year (12).

A few years ago, I was involved in a subsea survey of the Mediterranean between Spain and North Africa. The seabed close to Europe was relatively rubbish free. The closer we got to North Africa the more rubbish appeared. When we arrived off the coast of Algeria we could see rubbish trucks dumping directly into the sea. Ninety percent of the pollution in the sea is plastic based.

Plastic dumping, particularly in the Third World, is killing the world's oceans but it's only the Western countries that the UN seeks to financially penalise. The UN is so busy redistributing wealth that they ignore the small fact that the sea is being destroyed by the Third World (13).

The Great Pacific Garbage Patch is located in the North Pacific Gyre off the coast of California and is the largest ocean garbage site in the world. Studies show that the plastics found here come mostly from Africa. This microplastic soup is twice the size of Texas. The small pieces of plastic cannot be seen from the air and are far more dangerous to marine life as they are regularly ingested.

One million sea birds and 100,000 marine mammals are killed annually from plastic in our oceans. Forty-four percent of all sea bird species, 22 percent of cetaceans, all sea turtle species and a growing list of fish species have been documented with plastic in or around their bodies.

Plastic chemicals can be absorbed by the human body. Ninety-three percent of Americans aged six or older test positive for BPA, which is a plastic chemical. (14)

GREENPEACE ABANDONS GAIA

When, as a commercial diver and welder, I fought for Greenpeace, Patrick Moore was our president. Under his leadership, we were the 'Warriors of the Rainbow' and read 'Black Elk Speaks' on our bunks. Like American Indians, we risked our lives in the belief that we were a part of the life of the Earth. We wanted to save our planet and we still believed that we were a part of it.

Professor James Lovelock and Lynn Margulis wrote a book in the 70s that suggested that Planet Earth is a living organism. The Gaia Theory, as it came to be known, suggests that the Earth is a self-regulating complex system of which we are an integral part.

And then came Al Gore!

HOW TO SAVE A PLANET NEAR YOU!

Learn from history! Protest is pointless! As we proved in the 1980s, it is often counter-productive. We should have been a lot more careful of the monsters we woke up!

By the early 1990s we knew that the Green Movement was in trouble. The 'Big State' stopped fighting us at the exact time that they started using our cause against us.

By the mid 1990s humans were no longer 'Warriors of the Rainbow' but had now become the enemies of the Earth. Why? Because Cultural Marxism had completely taken over the Green Movement and science was ditched in favour of scaring the shit out of people and furthering the communist agenda.

Cultural Marxism, like Judeo/Christianity sees human life as separate and external to the Gaia organism, rather than as an integral part of it. Neither does Cultural Marxism have any faith in anything other than its own right to dominate the world.

Today's UK Green Party intends to build half a million homes on greenbelt land and pay everyone to do nothing.

IT WASN'T ALWAYS LIKE THIS!

Green politics had originally been an incredibly radical idea that would have created unity and reduced consumption, but it would also have meant turning the clock back on the industrial revolution. If real Green Politics had not been subverted by the one-world government we could have eradicated the consumerist society that is now killing the planet.

Unfortunately, with Al Gore's help, the people were distracted with the story of Global Warming. With bells and whistles and Hollywood movies, the big state made the people look at exactly what they wanted them to look at. They buried our dream of Gaia under an avalanche of fear, lies and fake science.

Like sheep in a field, we all went back to consuming. Only now, we had foolishly created a new way for the one-world government to suck money out of the people. Gore's carbon tax ended up hurting the most vulnerable people on the planet and making him a multimillionaire at the same time.

So this is why I say that "Protest is Pointless!"

Every time we try to force the world into our own idea of how it should be we always end up making things worse. In my experience, the only way to change the world is to change one's self.

The only real way that you can save the planet is to make your life an example that everyone else will want to follow for themselves. If you feel any urge toward using coercion, you are thinking with the 'Self of Now' and you are doomed to create even more suffering.

A WORLD IN DARKNESS

How did our world get to the point where people don't care how they treat animals?

When did it become OK for multinational companies to poison the world's population and contaminate the food chain?

When did our government decide that we were their enemies?

When did governments stop protecting the people? When did it become so common for people to treat each other so badly?

All of these terrible things are just symptoms of the corrosive worldview that has been forced upon us. Every attempt to deal with any of those symptoms will only make things worse if it is done in the context of the same worldview.

Try to force people to be polite and you end up destroying free speech. All of our best intentions take us further into the darkness.

Protest becomes rebellion and rebellion becomes war and the freedom fighters become the new tyrants. Like Pol Pot, Mao and Stalin, in trying to make things better we might cost millions of people their lives.

The Cultural Marxist narrative tells us that all of this horror is the fault of humans and in particular 'white Northern European men' but that is an oversimplification that plays into the hands of the state. If they can divide us they can control us!

Deer, if left to their own devices, will destroy their environment and move on. Does this make the deer a virus on the body of the Earth? No, of course not!

Human beings are constructed from the 'stuff' of the Earth. Imagine that the Earth is a sea made of soil, we are just waves within that soil. History has shown that the Earth is a self-regulating organism.

We need to have faith in a system that we are all a part of. We can leave tomorrow to Gaia, because there is a middle way!

BECOME A LIGHT TO THE WORLD

If you change your inner life so that these evils could never take root in your mind, you will find that your light will change the people around you. In this way, one person can change the world.

First change the direction of your heart and then allow it to change the way that you live your life.

Refuse to conform to a worldview just because it is fashionable. Refuse to be brainwashed and trust your common sense. Be prepared to truly be a spiritual warrior of the rainbow and you will change the world naturally. As you change as a person, so will the world around you.

LUNCH AT THE SOUL BAR

After three days of travelling, I was glad to have some time to rest before the start of the offshore project.

Walking into the Soul Bar at midday was like coming home to mother.

The Soul Bar is probably one of the most remarkable bars in Scotland. Predictably enough, it's a converted church built in a mock gothic style. Stained glass windows and soft varnished wood are all that's left of the brimstone and eternal damnation that was preached every day for a hundred and forty years.

As I looked at the menu I couldn't help thinking of Vicci and wondered if she was okay. Life is something that happens to us while we are busy planning to do something else. I couldn't help laughing at the young man I had once been! So serious, so fatally romantic and so pretentious.

Looking at the pews that still line the outside of the church, I wondered about the people whose bodies had polished the wood with their lives. Those lives were so narrow and grey simply because they kept themselves away from everyone who didn't share their view of the world.

They were forbidden to have any contact with Catholics; just as the Turks and the Kurds kept themselves separate from their Christian Armenian neighbours.

It is that separation that allows the 'Self of Now' to project onto an entire people the demons that live within our own minds.

As I sipped a glass of wine I realised that my life had given me a unique perspective. Constant world travel had made me a citizen of nowhere but at the same time of everywhere.

It may have been exhaustion or it may have been a revelation but for a few moments the six directions merge into infinity. The past and the future dissolve into meaningless concepts.

I could see that all life is just a wave within the sea of matter that forms the surface of our planet.

From the Caspian to the North Sea, it is only the illusion of the self that has created all of the suffering of the world.

Looking up at the pulpit I wondered how many men over all those years had presumed to speak for God.

People love priests, saviours and masters but I could see from this strange perspective that life is an infinite spiral and there really are no masters.

Standing on this spiral there really are no saviours, only us. All we have is each other.

Because reality is an infinite spiral, if you think that you are at the top it only means that, instead of looking up, you are just looking down toward the 'Self of Now'.

It was in the Soul Bar in Aberdeen that I realised that I had to share this vision with the world. Not because my vision was unique, rather specifically because it belonged to every person that ever has, or ever will, live.

CHAPTER 15

****

TEN RULES FOR LIVING WITHIN THE MATRIX

Two days in Aberdeen can seem like a lifetime. We still had no sign of a boat and I was certain now that the project would be shelved. I had used the time to try to make sense of my new understanding of the Holistic Universe.

I had spent the day walking. Almost by accident, I found myself on the northern pier of the harbour looking out into the brown North Sea beneath a sky that looked like it was made of steel and steam.

It felt like my journey was over and I was just waiting for my life to catch up! Aberdeen can do that to a man.

This journey that we've shared from the Caspian to the North Sea has seen both of us grow.

My vision shifted and instead of seeing the clouds stained red by the dying sun, I saw the spider's web of the sub-atomic universe within the last of the light. I realised that the world we live in is the one that we choose to see.

Like the brightly coloured Easter decorations in Union Street, religions and New-Age spirituality offer us a view of the world that we might choose to believe in but these are not worlds we can ever really know or confirm for ourselves.

The Holistic Universe gives us a way to see a different kind of world and know it for ourselves.

When we live within the darkness we forget what light even looks like. When you finally make some room in your life for the light, you will probably wonder how you ever lived as you did.

If you are anything like me, you will regret all the wasted years. With that in mind, I wanted to leave you with these ten laws, in the hope that they might help you avoid some of the pain that my stupidity caused me and everyone around me.

1. EVERY DAY IS AN OPPORTUNITY TO ACHIEVE YOUR SOUL'S PURPOSE:

The only time you can change is now! Remember that the world you see is a reflection of your 'Self of Now' and is therefore a clue as to what you need to change in your life.

We all have a reason to be alive. Where you find your joy, your fulfilment, that is your soul's purpose.

That doesn't mean that we all have to become opera singers or artists.

There used to be a street sweeper in my village. He had fought in too many wars and had once been a schoolteacher. Every day you would find him lost in concentration as he put all of himself into being the best street sweeper in the world. He was always full of joy and he enriched everyone who was ever lucky enough to meet him. His soul's purpose was to sweep the streets and that was fine.

2. LEARN TO LISTEN TO THE UNIVERSE:

Unless you learn to stop talking in your head, you will never hear the quiet voice within. Therefore, the greatest gift that the QM4YS system can give you is the ability to listen to silence.

You will see that when you are full of yourself, there's just no room for anything else in your life, the world will not be enough. On the other hand, if you learn to let go of your idea of yourself, you will find that there's more than enough room to fit the entire universe within your heart.

When you know how to listen you will find that the universe is always talking to you. Within the tiniest of things you will feel surrounded by the love of the universe.

3. THE NEGATIVE THINGS YOU SEE ARE REFLECTIONS OF YOUR 'SELF OF NOW':

Many people go through their lives just looking for things to be 'offended' about. The more they can find things 'out there' to set themselves against, the more the 'Self of Now' feels its own reality vindicated.

Resist your urge to be offended. Rather, take the time to notice what it is that pulled your trigger. Usually, that thing that annoys you will be a mirror of something inside yourself.

4. EVERYDAY TAKE THE TIME TO NOTICE THAT THE UNIVERSE CONSPIRES TO GIVE YOU EXACTLY WHAT YOU NEED TO GROW:

Take the time to smell the flowers! Notice how supported you are by life. Develop a sense of gratitude to protect you when times get rough.

Every morning when you wake start your day by thinking of all the things you are grateful for. When you start, you may not find anything but if you keep up with the practice you will find that you are grateful for the air you breathe.

5. EVERYTHING IN YOUR LIFE IS A TEST:

The Holistic Universe seeks balance. Growth is a spiral. What often feels like a setback is often the best thing that could happen.

Face the difficulties with the knowledge that you are a unique part of an infinite universe. Everything that happens does so for a reason.

Dark Matter can only work upon the 'Self of Now'. The 'Self of Now' is the causation of Dark Matter and it is the only one who suffers. If you can learn to let go of this illusion you will find the power to transcend suffering and death.

6. LIVE WITH JOY:

When you change the direction of your intention outward toward the Holistic Universe your sense of 'Self of Now' dissolves and you begin to live with the joy that is the very essence of yourself. You will find a deep joy in every part of your life and even the bad times will come to make sense.

Only by being 100% involved in life will you ever really become everything you need to be. Strive to be authentic.

Ironically, the 'Self of Now' only exists within the past and future. If you can learn to anchor yourself in this very moment then you will find joy is your constant companion. Strive to always be awake to the present moment and you won't have to search for joy because you will realise that it was with you all the time.

7. IF YOU THINK YOU KNOW IT ALL, YOU HAVE UNDERSTOOD NOTHING:

The 'Self of Now' will try to convince you that you have all the answers and that your new found spiritual knowledge makes you superior to other people.

Forget it! Everyone has a direct access to the Holistic Universe and everyone expresses it as best they can. Their truth is as valid as yours.

If you are going in the right direction you will begin to only judge other people through the prism of your own weakness. When you feel like you know it all you actually have nothing.

There is no such thing as 'enlightenment' for you to attain, nor is there any mystical experience that will save you from life.

8. CONSTANTLY EXAMINE YOUR OWN INNER LIFE:

Learn to treasure silence. Enjoy being alone. Practice introspection and always be open to new ideas. Attach your 'Self of Now' to 'no-thing' but, at the same time, treasure everything as an infinitely precious expression of the universe.

When you learn to watch the stream of your own inner life you will notice all of the things that your 'Self of Now' has been keeping hidden. You will notice that most of your previous life has been lived only for yourself.

The closer you get to the light the more you will be tested. Only through constantly being mindful of our own inner life can we continue our own spiritual evolution and forward movement.

9. MAKE DEATH YOUR TEACHER:

We live our lives as though we will live forever. We treat people as though they were snap shots of reality. Live each day as if it were your last.

Use your mortality to infuse every moment of your life with an infinite sweetness.

'May you live forever' is an ancient Greek curse. If life had no death it would lose all of its sweetness and meaning.

When we make death our teacher and live each day as if it were our last, we are finally truly immersed in the game of life. Colours will seem brighter, music sweeter and laughter more full of light.

You will learn to pity those people that live their lives with eyes firmly fixed on a next life that will never ever come. You will know in your heart and in your bones that now is all there ever will be.

10. NEVER JUDGE OTHERS:

Every time we judge other people we coagulate our sense of the 'Self of Now'. We give the Darkness something to act upon. The judgements we project onto other people exist first within us, so we therefore invite the universe to bring that Darkness onto us.

The very worst thing you can do in life is to judge other people.

If you find that your life is presenting you with divisions — if your mind is always coming up with reasons why person 'X' is different from you — this is the universe warning you that you are going in the wrong direction.

If you find that you can always find a way to see the other person's point of view — if you find that you can see why people do and say the things they do — if you find that your life is bringing you closer toward unity this is a very good sign that you are headed in the right direction.

GOODBYE TO ABERDEEN

I walked past the old lighthouse as the sun was falling and the afternoon quickly turned from freezing to an Arctic cold that burnt my lungs. I thought of the book that I would have to write and wondered if I had the skill to do this message justice.

I walked up to a bookshop on Union Street to hide from the cold and rode the elevator to its cafe. In all of these shiny self-help books there is a kind of truth. They are not entirely wrong but they can never be totally right because they belong to someone else.

I decided that I would have to write a book that was firmly bolted down to the ground. I didn't want to write yet another esoteric tome that gives the reader nothing to take away. I didn't want to be just another 'New Age' guru, prophet or teacher whose videos you watch or whose books you read but quickly forget.

You know the ones? You crave the daily dose of spiritual Kool-Aid but never actually change your self.

You buy their new book or the inevitable guided meditation and, for a little while, you feel some kind of a connection but that high soon wears off.

I would rather kill myself than be just another empty placebo for the spirituality and connection that you truly long for. I wanted more for you than that.

And now that dream is real and the book is nearly finished.

Now that you've read the best that I could give you, I hope that you've enjoyed this time we've spent together and more than anything I hope that you might find within this book a reason to wake-up and transcend the world that was built to keep you enslaved.

I'm hoping that you can now see why more 'Self' is probably the worst thing you can buy, if you want to sort your life out.

It's a cliché, I know, but it's true that the world is on a cusp and everything is hanging in balance. It is now up to you to apply these insights into your own life. You now have the chance to repair yourself and by so doing, you will change the world.

If I've done my job properly, you will now see how suffering is caused and how you can begin to avoid it. More than anything it is my hope that you will now have a good reason to believe in your own intuition and common sense.

If you have any questions or constructive feedback, please don't hesitate to contact me directly through the website. Before I go, don't forget you will need your gift code in order to claim your free copy of the foundation course:

Foundation Course Code: **Duka1892**

www.howdoifixme.com

✳✳✳✳

CHAPTER 16

REFERENCES AND CHAPTER NOTES

CHAPTER 1

1. https://academic.oup.com/brain/article/132/5/1396/354862

2. The Black Book of Communism: Crimes, Terror, Repression is a 1997 book edited by Stéphane Courtois. Also see http://reason.com/blog/2013/03/13/communism-killed-94m-in-20th-century.

3. https://medical-dictionary.thefreedictionary.com/Transference+(psychology)

4. Halton Arp was an American astronomer who dared to question the two assumptions upon which the Big Bang Theory is based. He demonstrated that planetary 'Red Shifts' cannot be used as an indication of distance or speed of recession. He speculated that some other factor is changing the frequency of light. (https://www.nytimes.com/2014/01/07/science/space/halton-c-arp-astronomer-who-challenged-big-bang-theory-dies-at-86.html). He was initially asked to suppress his findings and was not allowed to publish. Eventually his career was ruined because he asked the wrong questions.

•   Dr Judith Curry was bullied out of her position as professor and former chair of the school of Earth and Atmospheric Sciences at the Georgia Institute of Technology because she dared to question the scientific dogma that insists that CO_2 drives global temperature and that man-made CO_2 is responsible for changes in global weather.(From her 'The State of the Climate Debate' in 2015' and http://www.climatedepot.com/2017/01/03/craziness-in-climate-field-leads-dissenter-dr-judith-curry-to-resign-i-have-resigned-my-tenured-faculty-position-at-georgia-tech)

CHAPTER 2

1. Paul Johnson's book 'Intellectuals' 1988 exposes the character of Marx. http://biography.yourdictionary.com/karl-marx

2. The Black Book of Communism: Crimes, Terror, Repression is a 1997 book edited by Stéphane Courtois. Also see http://reason.com/blog/2013/03/13/communism-killed-94m-in-20th-century

CHAPTER 3

1. http://www.armenian-genocide.org/

2. http://endgenocide.org/learn/past-genocides/the-cambodian-genocide/

3. http://www.breitbart.com/london/2016/09/14/massive-cover-exposed-lying-alarmists-rebranded-70s-global-cooling-scare-myth/

4. http://www.medicalbag.com/despicable-doctors/walter-freeman-the-father-of-the-lobotomy/article/472966/

5. http://www.stopshrinks.org/reading_room/drugs/dark_side_1.htm

6. https://breggin.com/

7. https://thepolicy.us/cultural-marxism-the-origins-of-the-present-day-social-justice-movement-and-political-correctness-ffb89c6ef4f1

8. David Berlinski Ph.D - The Deniable Darwin and Other Essays

9. Professor Jonathan Wells - Icons of Evolution: Science or Myth: Why Much of What We Teach About Evolution Is Wrong. Zombie Science: more icons of evolution

10. https://www.nyu.edu/projects/sanger/webedition/app/documents/show.php?sangerDoc=238946.xml

CHAPTER 4

1. Professor Rupert Sheldrake - The Science Delusion

2. http://www.iflscience.com/brain/long-term-memories-may-not-be-stored-synapses-afterall/

3. https://www.naturalnews.com/042260_genetics_myths_Human_Genome_Project_morphic_resonance.html. Also See Sheldrake as No 1.

CHAPTER 6

1. http://www.bbc.com/news/world-asia-india-27775327

CHAPTER 7

1. https://www.youtube.com/watch?v=PolFadm-lgU

2. Nikola Tesla: Imagination and the Man That Invented the 20th Century by Sean Patrick

3. Bill Gaede - The Rope Hypothesis 342

4. http://thehistoryoftheatom.weebly.com/lord-rutherford.html

5. http://thehistoryoftheatom.weebly.com/niels-bohr.html

6. Bill Gaede

7. Bill Gaede - The Rope Hypothesis 342

8. https://www.bell-labs.com/explore/stories-changed-world/Cosmic-Microwave-Background-Discovery/

9. Bill Gaede - How a magnet physically attracts another from a distance 344

10. https://www.youtube.com/watch?v=RQnw5KyLNx4

11. Ken L. Wheeler - Uncovering the Missing Secrets of magnetism

CHAPTER 8

1. Geral Winer Ohio State University - reference from the Science Delusion below.

2. Professor Rupert Sheldrake - The Science Delusion. References a paper by Sir Rudolph Peters formally professor of biochemistry at Oxford.https://www.ncbi.nlm.nih.gov/pmc/articles/PMC3202497/

3. https://www.youtube.com/watch?v=aAJkLh76QnM&t=154s

4. https://www.youtube.com/watch?v=snnmlqz_UCc

5. Dr Suzanne Simard: https://e360.yale.edu/features/exploring_how_and_why_trees_talk_to_each_other

CHAPTER 9

1. https://www.youtube.com/watch?v=hogBsRSJdcs

2. https://www.psychologytoday.com/blog/under-the-influence/201307/diogenes-influence-personality

3. https://www.theguardian.com/science/2000/jun/26/genetics13

4. https://www.europhysicsnews.org/articles/epn/pdf/2015/02/epn2015462p26.pdf

5. https://www.sciencedaily.com/releases/2016/08/160825113235.htm

CHAPTER 10

1. http://www.buddhistdoor.com/OldWeb/bdoor/archive/nutshell/teach9.htm

2. https://www.space.com/20930-dark-matter.html

3. http://www.nanomotion.com/piezo-ceramic-motor-technology/piezoelectric-effect/

4. http://www.nature.com/news/2004/041220/full/news041220-6.html

5. https://www.youtube.com/watch?v=aAJkLh76QnM

6. Charles Manson: https://www.youtube.com/watch?v=StK3oFcLWeU

CHAPTER 11

1. https://www.cs.cmu.edu/~dst/OTIII/spaink-ot3.html

2. Peter R Breggin, MD - Guilt, Shame and Anxiety: understanding and overcoming Negative Emotions.

CHAPTER 12

1. The Body Electric: electromagnetism and the foundation of life by Robert O. Becker MD and Gary Selden.

CHAPTER 14

1. http://ic.galegroup.com Science in Context: Factory Farming by Susan Aldridge 2011.

2. https://www.peta.org/issues/animals-used-for-food/factory-farming/chickens/chicken-industry/

3. https://www.peta.org/issues/animals-used-for-food/factory-farming/cows/dairy-industry/

4. https://www.peta.org/issues/animals-used-for-food/factory-farming/pigs/pork-industry/

5. https://www.scientificamerican.com/article/how-drug-resistant-bacteria-travel-from-the-farm-to-your-table/

6. https://www.peta.org/features/top-five-shocking-animal-experimentation-facts/

7. https://www.globalresearch.ca/the-complete-history-of-monsanto-the-worlds-most-evil-corporation/5387964

8. http://www.un.org/apps/news/story.asp?NewsID=48342#.WiPIKIW5CsM

9. http://www.mindbodyhealth.com/avoidsoy.htm

10. Dr Thierry Vrain, a former Pro-GMO Scientist, refutes the claims of the biotechnology companies - https://foodrevolution.org/blog/former-pro-gmo-scientist/ and - http://nutritionstudies.org/gmo-dangers-facts-you-need-to-know/

11. https://www.naturalnews.com/041766_aspartame_GM_bacteria_patent.html

12. http://oceancrusaders.org/plastic-crusades/plastic-statistics/

13. https://weather.com/science/weather-explainers/news/ocean-currents-eddies-temperature-images

14. http://www.businessinsider.com/facts-bottled-water-industry-2011-10?op=1/#e-2011-global-forecast-called-for-over-86-billion-in-profits-14

****

IMAGE INDEX

- *Image 5: Louis De Broglie's model of the atom*

- *Image 6: Shrodinger and Born probability model of the atom.*

- *Image 7: EM Rope model of the atom*

- *Image 8: EM Rope model of electromagnetic Aether*

- *Image 9: EM Rope model of local magnetic attraction.*

- *Image 10: Einstein's curved space explanation for planetary orbit.*

- *Image 11: EM Rope model of planetary orbit*

- *Image 12: Thomas Young's famous slit experiment*

- *Image 13: Young's assumption of lightwave interference patterns.*

- *Image 14: Einstein's light-as-a-particle explanation for 'fringes'.*

- *Image 15: Light bent by the assumed curvature of space.*

- *Image 16: observed reality — light bends around corners.*

- *Image 17: Gaede's Needle experiment single object creating fringes.*

- *Image 18: Individual and group resonant fields.*

- *Image 19: GDV clinical diagnostic image.*

- *Image 20: Photo of gold atom from Brookhaven.*

- *Image 21: Fibonacci sequence perfection of form.*

- *Image 22: Dark Matter visualisation.*

- *Image 23: 'Self of Now' creates Dark Matter.*

- *Image 24: Piezoelectric effect on organic material.*

- *Image 25: Formation of Dark Crystal by Dark Matter.*

- *Image 26: Chaos Theory — Strange Attractors.*

- *Image 27: Distortions in the Dark Crystal.*

- *Image 28: Symbol of the Holistic Universe.*

- *Image 29: QM4YS Sacred Hoop.*

- *Image 30: Changing the direction of intention.*

- *Image 31: QM4YS System of Self-Repair.*

- *Image 32: Shang, Zhong and Xia Dantians related to the Holistic Universe*

THE END

www.ingramcontent.com/pod-product-compliance
Lightning Source LLC
Chambersburg PA
CBHW071949090426
42740CB00011B/1865